Across the Board

Building Academic Reading Skills

D0033324

Jean Zukowski/Faust

Northern Arizona University

THOMSON LEARNING   Australia • Canada • Mexico • Singapore • Spain • United Kingdom • United States

Across the Board
Building Academic Reading Skills
Jean Zukowski/Faust

Developmental Editor: *Phyllis Dobbins*
Production Editor: *Angela Williams Urquhart*
Marketing Manager: *Katrina Byrd*
Manufacturing Coordinator: *Holly Mason*
Production/Composition: *Real Media Solutions*

Copy Editor: *Dina Forbes, WordPlayers*
Cover Designer: *Bill Brammer Design*
Printer: *Webcom*

Printed in Canada.
1 2 3 4 5 6 7 8 9 10 06 05 04 03 02 01

For more information contact Heinle & Heinle, 25 Thomson Place, Boston, Massachusetts 02210 USA, or you can visit our Internet site at http://www.heinle.com

For permission to use material from this text or product, contact us:
Tel   1-800-730-2214
Fax   1-800-730-2215
Web http://www.thomsonrights.com

Library of Congress Control Number: 2001095320
ISBN: 0-03-032482-3

Photo Credits: Page 1: Monica Lau/PhotoDisc; Pages 51, 53, 54, 141, 145, 193, 195, 196, and 197: Helen Zukowski; Pages 65, 67, and 68: Katy Archer; Page 83: Bert Hardy/©Hulton-Deutsch Collection/Corbis; Page 173: Arthur S. Aubry/PhotoDisc; Page 176: Janis Christie/PhotoDisc; Pages 211 and 213: Doug Menuez/PhotoDisc; Pages 229 and 233: Bettmann/Corbis; Pages 245, 247, and 249: Chris Giannola; all other photos provided by John and Jean Zukowski/Faust

Contents

Introduction

This book for English language readers is designed to help your students develop familiarity with the lexis and idiom of the major human topics within human experience. Reading is interaction with a text. Therefore, toward the goal of strengthening vocabulary at the intermediate level, the stories in this book are written to relate to human experience and offer opportunity for enjoyment of both wonderful and terrible things in other people's lives.

What will you find in this book?

There are 15 true stories in this book. They are told in first and third person from the perspectives of a mother, a daughter, a son, and a father. An effort has been made to use and recycle the everyday vocabulary related to these fields: home, marriage and family relationships; work, jobs, and occupations; animals and farm life; survival skills; community involvement; spirituality and mysticism; government and law; crime and violence; ceremony; communication; education; transportation and driving; science; psychology and mental health; nature; environmentalism; eating and cooking; suffering, dying, and death; time and space; technology; medicine, hospitals, and health; ethics; common sense; and economics.

You will find that there are some areas (like sports, popular music, entertainment, and fashion) that are not strongly represented in this book. It is the experience of the writer that these topics, as elements of current and ever-changing popularity for your students, need little academic reinforcement.

What is the vocabulary level?

In the main, the vocabulary in this book is basic. Some words that are very easy to learn and add interest and color to a story are also included. The grade level on common readability scales measures between 3.2 and 5.2 on the readings themselves. The level of measured difficulty might vary with the types of exercises that are included in each unit, to help your students hone the component reading skills of a good reader. In the back of the book, there is an alphabetical list of the focus words from each unit. The word is identified as a noun (*n*), verb (*v*) regular or irregular with the principal parts of irregular verbs given, adjective (*adj*), and adverb (*adv*). The story in which the word appears as a focus word is also noted. You will find that the Vocabulary List includes more words that are target words in the lessons. For example, there are words used in directions that have been listed in the Vocabulary List. The Vocabulary List can help you find topics of immediate relevance in your classes.

What is the level of the readings?

The readings vary in length from 700 to 1,500 words. The skills focuses are on understanding the text. Students are also asked to practice the academic skills of finding the main idea, making inferences, and drawing conclusions. They are asked to figure out meanings of idioms from context and what the relationships between words or concepts are.

Vocabulary expansion is a natural emphasis for students at this high-beginning, low-intermediate level of English language development. However, because so much of what is found in the stories reflects realities of students' own lives, many students will be able to read far beyond their actual measured level of comprehension and language production. Such expansion of their skills should be encouraged.

How is vocabulary presented?

Words that might be vaguely familiar or unfamiliar to the students are glossed in a Words and Idioms List in each unit of the book. You are encouraged to go over these meanings with your students. However, it is far better for students to read without making reference to the Words and Idioms List, so that they develop their natural feelings for the meanings of the words rather than memorize definitions. Note that idioms are included here to assist students' understanding.

Idioms have to be learned in multiple contexts before they can be used naturally. In general you may want to avoid asking students to try to use the idioms in sentences, but rather you can include the use of these idioms in your speech as much as is natural for you. Students of language have to hear and see these idioms in use to form a clear sense of language experience with the phrases.

How can variety be introduced into the presentation of the lessons?

For ease of reference, the units are arranged following a similar style and template. However, many students will fare far better if your teaching approach to the story is varied.

Sometimes you might read the whole story aloud to the class while the students' books remain closed. Other times you might want to have the students begin by guessing what, judging from the title and graphics alone, might be in the story. A lesson might begin with a discussion question gleaned from the story. On another occasion, you might start with a focus on the new words and idioms. A fourth option is to begin with a brainstorm of words and ideas that one expects from a story about a specific topic. The topic of driving, in "The Day Anna Kadulski Learned to Drive," for example, can be used to generate a list of words related to automobiles, traffic, and driver's license processes. In any case, you are likely to find that a varied approach works best.

You will note that there are exercises that work well as quick reviews of vocabulary meaning and plenty to select from for homework. Pick, vary, choose, and above all, enjoy!

Acknowledgments

Special thanks to Phyllis Dobbins, Carolyn Martin, and Angela Urquhart of Heinle and Heinle; Elizabeth Geary, Robert Bovasso, and Conni Wynn-Smith of Real Media Solutions; and Dina Forbes and Jacqueline Flamm of WordPlayers.

Because these stories are real stories, I must also thank members of the family who have helped me with them: my husband John and my daughter Josie for their help in brainstorming and refining the family stories, my son Jonathan for his story of the Warsaw train station, and my mother Helen Zukowski for the story of her mother's driving lessons and her Aunt Agnes's wedding ring.

Angels for One Another

Every person is a story. What is the story behind the beauty of the woman from India? How could a person know that she needed an angel to help her?

Before You Read the Story

Use these questions as preparation for reading the story. If you need to know the meaning of a word or idiom, check the Words and Idioms List after the story.

1. What does the title mean to you?

2. The word *angel* means "messenger," or person who carries a message from one person to another. Usually we think of angels as messengers from heaven, but this angel is a helper. How do the angels help?

3. This story takes place in an airport waiting area. What do you know about such places? What do you find in a waiting lounge? How do people usually act in an airport lounge?

While You Read the Story

Read these questions and look for the answers as you read the story.

1. Who are the main characters in the story?

2. Which person in the story talked the most?

3. What had happened to the family from India?

4. Why did they need an angel?

Angels for One Another

1   I was on my way home to Arizona from Turkey. I had a four-hour layover in Frankfurt. But waiting was no problem. I had books to read and letters to write. First I checked with the airline for the place and time of departure.

5   And I went to the lounge of the departure area. The airport was crowded that day, but I saw one row of five connected seats. That row looked empty at first, but then I realized it wasn't. A long red duffel bag lay across

10   three of the seats. I took the seat at the other end.

About fifteen minutes later, I saw a beautiful young Indian woman coming toward me. She had a baby in her arms and two young girls at her side. The oldest of the three children,

15   a girl of about seven, was looking straight at me. And she had daggers in her eyes. She stared at me with anger until she sat down on the floor next to me. She opened a small bag and took out a beautiful white lace heart. It had been crocheted by hand. She took a pair of scissors out of the

20   knapsack, and she was just about to drive the scissors into the heart. I spoke up, "That's the way to ruin that lovely heart." She turned and looked at me. "Someone who loves you must have made it for you," I said.

"My grandmother made it," she said. She put down the

25   scissors.

The baby boy was coughing and crying. He was obviously sick, and the mother was busy taking care of him. She glanced at her daughters and at me. She looked tired and unhappy. Then the seven-year-old reached into the knapsack.

30 She pulled out a lovely piece of handmade lace. It was a long strip, perhaps four meters in length. It was sewn to a long piece of cloth; perhaps it had been cut from the bottom of a dress. She reached for the scissors again. I spoke again. "What pretty lace!" I said. "You could make something out of it."

35 The little girl and her three-year-old sister looked at me. To them it was nothing. I showed them how, by working together, we could separate the lace from the cloth. For more than an hour, we worked. Stitch by stitch we freed the lace. And we talked. They were going to Cincinnati, like I was. 40 They lived in Indiana. Their father worked there. They had been in India for their uncle's wedding. I turned to their mother; she and the baby were both asleep. We finished with the lace, and then Sara took a book out of the bag. Her little sister climbed onto my lap, and together we read the book. 45 Ama fell asleep in my arms, but Sara talked on.

The baby awoke, and the mother did too. She watched her daughters and me for a while. Then she introduced herself as Chandra. I told her that my name was Jean. And she thanked me for letting her have a few moments of rest. Then 50 she asked if she could leave her daughters with me for a few minutes. She needed to change the baby's diaper. It was no problem for me. The girls seemed comfortable, and I was enjoying their company. The baby fell back asleep after they returned. Then the girls and I went to wash our hands and 55 comb our hair. And then we were all back together in the waiting room.

Suddenly Sara looked up at me and said, "They tried to kill Grandma." I was obviously shocked by her words. I glanced at her mother.

60   The mother said, "That's right." And then the three of them told me their story. They had gone to India for the wedding of the girls' uncle. It was a very big celebration for a very important family. Three hundred guests were coming. The

65   house was painted inside and out. The family treasures were taken out of the bank vault for the occasion. New servants were hired too. One of the new workers was a new cook. The day after the wedding, the groom and bride left on a trip. Chandra and her children went with Grandfather in the car to

70   Delhi to catch the plane. It would take a full day to get there.

From the airport in Delhi, they called to say goodbye and heard this story.

The cook had put some poison, a sleeping medicine, in the food. Everyone who ate the food fell into a deep sleep.

75   Chandra's mother, sister, brother-in-law, the night guards, and all the other servants had fallen asleep. In the morning, the day guard came to the house. No one was there to open the gate. No one answered when he called. He went to the police. They found that all the wedding gifts were gone. All

80   the family treasures were missing. And everyone in the house was sound asleep, drugged. By noon everyone had awakened, except Grandma. They took her to the hospital and tried to wake her up, but she was still asleep. Nothing, it seemed, would wake her up.

85   Chandra asked if I would stay with the girls while she tried to telephone again. This time, she came back happy. Her mother was awake. She was still very sick, but she would be all right.

I asked, "Has she been in good health?"

90   Chandra replied, "Yes, she is still a young woman."

At that moment the announcement came over the public address system. They would be boarding our flight in fifteen minutes. I asked which seats they had. Chandra said, "Can you believe it? I am traveling halfway around the world with
95   three children, and I don't even have an aisle seat. We're in the middle three seats of row 23." My seat was next to theirs, on the end of the row. What a coincidence!

Then we returned to our conversation. Chandra mentioned that her mother's birthday had just passed, on April 3. So
100   had mine. In a few sentences we realized that her mother and I were born on exactly the same day. Chandra said, "I needed an angel, and you were sent to take my mother's place." Ama sat on my lap and slept all the way across the Atlantic, and Sara talked to me non-stop.

Words and Idioms List

You already know some of these words and idioms. Go through the list. Write a check (✓) next to each of those that you do not know.

Some of these words and idioms may be completely new for you. Find them in the reading. Use the sentences around them to understand what they mean. Note how they are used. These are the words and idioms to learn for this story.

1. _____   an **aisle seat** (noun): a place to sit next to the walkway

2. _____   an **angel** (noun): a heavenly creature, sent from God, to help

3. _____   a **bank vault** (noun): a safe; a locked-up place in a bank

4. _____   to **be shocked** (verb): to be surprised and unhappy

5. _____   **board a flight** (idiom): to be called by an airline employee to get onto an airplane before it leaves for its destination

6. _____ a **bride** (noun): a woman on her wedding day

7. _____ to **change a diaper** (idiom): to put a clean, dry covering on a baby

8. _____ a **coincidence** (noun): the happening of two things at the same time; an unusual event

9. _____ to **crochet** (verb): to use a special hooked tool to make thread or string into a pretty, net-like pattern

10. _____ **departure** (noun): an action of leaving from a place

11. _____ to **drive something into something else** (idiom): to force one thing into another

12. _____ **drugged** (adjective): under the influence of chemical substances

13. _____ a **duffel bag** (noun): a soft, usually long and round, bag for carrying clothing on a trip

14. _____ to **glance** (verb): to look quickly and then turn away

15. _____ a **groom** (noun): a man on his wedding day

16. _____ to **have daggers in one's eyes** (idiom): to look at someone in great anger

17. _____ **lace** (non-count noun): net-like crocheted trimming

18. _____ a **layover** (noun): a period of time between two airplane flights

19. _____ a **lounge** (noun): a sitting room

20. _____ **medicine** (non-count noun): chemical substances to help a sick person get better

21. _____ **non-stop** (adverb): without interruption

22. _____ a **poison** (noun): a chemical substance that can hurt people

23. _____ a **public address system** (noun): a loudspeaker system to give information

24. _____ to **ruin** (verb): to spoil; to break

25. _____ a **servant** (noun): a worker in one's home; a paid helper

26. _____ a **strip** (noun): a long and narrow piece

27. _____ **treasures** (plural noun): valuable things

28. _____ a **waiting room** (noun): a place with chairs, where people can wait for appointments

After You Have Read the Story

Do you have the answers to the questions from "While You Read the Story"? Talk about the answers with your classmates.

Understanding Sequence

In the blank in front of each sentence, write 2–12 to show that you know the order of the story.

a. _____ I saw a woman and three children coming toward the seats.

b. _____ She took out a crocheted heart and a pair of scissors.

c. __1__ I arrived in Frankfurt.

d. _____ I found out the departure area.

e. _____ We separated some lace from a strip of cloth.

f. _____ A little girl sat on the floor near me and opened a bag.

g. _____ We read a book together.

h. _____ I found a place to sit next to four empty seats with a red duffel bag on three of them.

i. _____ The girl and her mother told me the story of the wedding and the cook's actions.

j. _____ We got on the airplane to go to Cincinnati.

k. _____ I stopped her from ruining the heart.

l. _____ The woman went to telephone India and learned that her mother was all right.

Answering Questions About the Story

Read these questions, think about the answers, and then discuss the answers with your classmates.

1. Where did the Indian woman fly from to Frankfurt?
2. Where did Jean fly from?
3. Who made the crocheted heart?
4. Why was the woman tired? (Give more than one reason.)
5. Why was Sara angry?
6. Who was the angel?
7. Who was the groom?
8. Where was the groom two days after the wedding?

Drawing Conclusions from the Story

Which of these statements are probably true, from the information in the story? Write *true* or *false* in the blank in front of each sentence.

1. __*true*__ The new cook was the person who stole the wedding gifts.
2. _____ Chandra ate some of the food with poison in it.
3. _____ Chandra's family was very rich.
4. _____ Ama was the oldest child.
5. _____ Chandra and her children had a layover of more than four hours.
6. _____ The flight from India probably took longer than the flight from Turkey.
7. _____ Chandra's mother enjoyed making things by hand.
8. _____ The night guard ate more food than anyone else.
9. _____ Medicine can be a poison.
10. _____ A wedding is an important occasion for a family.

Finding the Meaning in Context

Which meaning is closest to the underlined word or words? Circle *a, b, c,* or *d.*

1. There is <u>a place to walk</u> between the stacks of things to buy in a store.
   a. a road
   b. an aisle
   c. a dagger
   d. a lounge

2. The family kept their valuable things in a <u>safe</u> in the bank.
   a. vault
   b. box
   c. duffel bag
   d. knapsack

3. What is the <u>time for the plane to leave</u>?
   a. boarding of the plane
   b. plane's departure
   c. non-stop
   d. to change a flight

4. They are sitting in the <u>waiting room</u>.
   a. lounge
   b. strip
   c. public address system
   d. aisle seats

5. The dress has <u>pretty white trimming</u> on the collar.
   a. strip
   b. daggers
   c. lace
   d. angel

6. The woman was <u>surprised</u> by the bad news.
   a. poison
   b. ruined
   c. ruined
   d. shocked

Matching New Words and Meanings

Draw a line between the two words or phrases with similar meanings.

1.	waiting room	a.	spoil
2.	duffel bag	b.	poison
3.	something crocheted	c.	look
4.	bride	d.	lace
5.	end of a row	e.	lovely
6.	medicine	f.	knapsack
7.	ruin	g.	shocked
8.	pretty	h.	lounge
9.	glance	i.	aisle seat
10.	surprised	j.	groom

Practicing with Idioms

Find the idiom in the Words and Idioms List that means the same or almost the same as the underlined word or words and write the correct form of it in the blank.

1. She looked at me <u>with anger</u>. She looked at me with _*daggers in*_ _*her eyes*_ .

2. The baby was wet, so she needed to <u>do something to make him dry</u>. She needed to _____ .

3. The voice on the airline public address system said that it would soon be time for passengers to <u>get on the airplane</u>. It would soon be time for passengers to _____ .

4. The man used a large hammer to <u>force the nail into the wall</u>. The man used a large hammer to _____ .

5. It is a good idea to keep valuable things in <u>a safe place in a bank</u>. It is a good idea to keep valuable things in _____ .

Exploring the Ideas

Think about these questions. Talk about your opinions with your classmates.

1. What is a *coincidence*?

2. Some people say that there are no coincidences. They believe things happen for a reason. How do you feel? Are there any coincidences in this story? What are they?

3. How was Jean like an angel?

4. Why didn't Chandra tell Jean the story immediately? How do you think you would have acted in the same situation?

5. How do we know that the children trusted Jean?

6. Why do you think Sara was going to drive the scissors into the white crocheted heart?

7. Why didn't Ama talk very much?

8. How do we know that Chandra trusted Jean?

Making Inferences

Read the numbered sentence. Then read the sentences under it. Which ones are true because the numbered sentence is true? Circle the letter in front of each statement that is probably true.

1. Sara looked at Jean with daggers in her eyes.

   a. Sara was very upset about something.

   b. Jean was a convenient person to be angry with.

   c. Sara didn't like the white crocheted heart.

   d. Sara didn't like her grandmother.

   e. Sara didn't know how to express her feelings.

2. Chandra looked very tired.

   a. Chandra had traveled a long way already with three children.

   b. Chandra didn't like traveling.

   c. Chandra was worried about her mother.

   d. Chandra didn't want to fly to Cincinnati until she knew about her mother.

   e. Chandra had a lot of work to do with a sick baby.

3. There were some coincidences.

    a. Both airplanes came to Frankfurt.

    b. Jean and Chandra's mother were born on the same day.

    c. Chandra had three tickets in the middle of a row on the airplane.

    d. Jean's seat was next to Chandra's seats.

    e. The baby was sick.

4. Sara wasn't really angry with Jean for sitting in the seat at the end of their row.

    a. Sara talked to Jean a lot.

    b. Sara told Jean the story about her grandmother.

    c. Sara let Jean show her how to work with the lace.

    d. Sara liked talking to someone.

5. The airplane was going to Cincinnati.

    a. Cincinnati must be in Arizona.

    b. Cincinnati must be in Indiana.

    c. Cincinnati must be an international airport.

    d. There must be planes to Arizona and Indiana from Cincinnati.

Finding the Main Ideas

Which title or titles are appropriate for this story? Circle the letter in front of each one.

a. The Wedding	e. A Seat on the Aisle
b. A Day in Frankfurt	f. A New Cook
c. Coincidences	g. On the Way to Cincinnati
d. Aunt Jean Helps	h. Talking in the Waiting Room

Reading for Details

Find the answers to these questions in the story.

1. What are the names of the people in Chandra's family?
2. What tool is mentioned that can cut?
3. How many guests came to the wedding?
4. How do we know that the family is rich?
5. Who put the poison in the food?
6. What is Delhi?
7. How long was Jean's layover?
8. Why did Chandra leave her children with a stranger?

Taking a Close Look at the Meanings of the Words

1. Look at the word *coincidence*. It is made up of two other word parts: *co* + *incidence*. *Co* means "together." An *incident* is a happening, an event. Two things that happen at the same time (and are related to each other) are *coincidental*.

2. *To lounge* means "to relax." Therefore, a *lounge* is a place to rest and relax. A *waiting room* is simply a place to wait.

3. Note that Sara picked up *a pair of scissors*. She put down the *scissors*. This tool has two parts, so it is called *a pair*, like *a pair of pants*, *a pair of socks*, or *a pair of gloves*. In common use, the words *a pair of* are often left out.

Lessons from the Farm

A farm may not look like a school. However, a young person can learn some important lessons for life on a farm.

Before You Read the Story

Use these questions as preparation for reading the story. If you need to know the meaning of a word or idiom, check the Words and Idioms List after the story.

1. What do you know about farms?
2. What are the common animals on a farm?
3. What kinds of work must people do on a farm?
4. In this story, the storyteller explains some of the lessons that she learned on the farm. What lessons do you think a young person would learn on a farm?

While You Read the Story

Read these questions and look for the answers as you read the story.

1. Who owned the farm?
2. Why did Uncle John need bean-pickers?
3. What happens on a farm before a bad storm? Why?
4. Why did the young people go to the farm?

Lessons from the Farm

1   I had never really lived on a farm, but my mother's Uncle John had a farm. So I spent time there, like all the other children in the family. The farm was just a few miles from town, so we could ride our bicycles there. Aunt Wanda, my

5   cousins, and the hired help all liked children. So we felt welcome there. Some very interesting things happened on that farm. I learned a lot about life and a lot about people there.

I learned about having a job and motivation. As we grew older, we were asked if we wanted to work on the farm. One

10   job that we all liked was picking beans. Uncle John planted several acres of green beans every spring, and in the middle of July, the beans were ready to begin picking. He drove his

yellow truck to town every morning and picked up his

15   bean-pickers. He made two stops, one at the park and one closer to our house. At seven in the morning, we children would be ready. We

20   had our buckets and paper sacks with our lunches. We wore light-colored long-sleeved shirts. We had big straw hats, too, to protect our heads from the sun. We were off to earn money for special things that we wanted.

25   Picking beans was not hard work. Each person took one row, knelt on a folded burlap sack, and pushed back the leaves. We were supposed to pluck the long green beans and put them in our pails. When a bucket was full, we emptied the beans into big clean burlap sacks. We called these bags gunnysacks.

30   A gunnysack could hold about 70 pounds of beans. Most days, we children each picked one bag full. We got paid for this work. Uncle John weighed the sacks at the end of the day. He deducted two pounds for the

35   weight of the sack. Aunt Wanda figured out how much we had earned and paid us three cents a pound.

Helen Miller was an adult who came with us sometimes. Mrs. Miller always picked more than 100 pounds. Some days she picked more than 200 pounds of beans. She didn't play,

40   however. My brothers always played, and they never got more than two dollars for the beans they picked. One day I chose a row next to Mrs. Miller's. I tried to work as fast as she did. That year I earned money for clothes and a gold wristwatch. It was good to separate work and play. We earned money, and

45   so did Uncle John. Every evening Uncle John took us back to town. Then he took the bags full of beans to a canning factory across the river.

One very hot day, at lunchtime, I learned another lesson. Uncle John suggested that we take a rest. The sun was simply

50   too strong for us to stay in the fields at high noon. My cousin Peggy and I went for a walk. Everything seemed quiet as we walked into the cool shady woods. We found a grassy place under a tree, stretched out, and fell sound asleep. I woke up suddenly. Someone was looking at me. I could feel eyes on me.

55   I looked up and saw no one. I sat up, and suddenly there was a great hullabaloo. Peggy woke up too, and we realized that a flock of 100 turkeys or more surrounded us. They wanted to be cool too. When we woke up, they were frightened. They were all raising their necks and gobble-gobbling at us.

60   The din was terrifying.

Peggy started to cry. It was frightening, all those turkeys! I don't know why, but I made a sound in response. I forced air out of my lungs and let my tongue make a flapping "R" sound. The turkeys suddenly all became quiet and settled down into the grass. Peggy got to her feet, and so did I! We needed to escape from all the turkeys. I continued making the whirring sound, and the turkeys stayed down. When I stopped, they started gobbling again. Later I learned that turkeys naturally fear hawks, and the whirring sound was like the sound of hawks' wings! Peggy laughed about my knowing how to talk to turkeys. It was an insight into learning to speak foreign languages.

There was one other important lesson that I learned on the farm. It was a warm Saturday morning in autumn. The fall colors were bright on the trees. My brother Ted and I had ridden our bicycles out to the farm to spend the day. We would help if we could. Suddenly, the sky grew dark, and the wind began to blow. It was obvious to us all that there was going to be a thunderstorm. Uncle John was leading his horses into their stalls in the barn. He called to us to help get the animals into the barn. Ted and I took up the sticks.

We ran to the meadow and started to move the small herd of cows toward the barn. The cows went willingly into the safety of the large building. All the cows—except for a yearling, that is—went peacefully into the barn. This young animal was stubbornly refusing to go in. Uncle John and Dan, his adult son, were both pulling on the rope around the calf's neck, and the animal's hooves were firmly planted in the earth ten feet from the door of the barn. Nothing, it seemed, would get that animal into the barn.

Ted watched and then asked, "Can I try?" Uncle John and Dan looked at him. Ted was only twelve years old. He was tall for his age, but he was certainly not as strong as Uncle John and Dan. Uncle John laughed and said, "OK, Teddy.

95 Have a go at it!" He threw the rope to Ted, who did not take it. Instead, Ted pulled hard on the tail of the calf, and the animal bolted straight into the barn. I learned that common sense is not common. I also learned that it is good to stop and think about something difficult to do. Sometimes it is

100 better to use one's brain instead of one's brawn.

Words and Idioms List

You already know some of these words and idioms. Go through the list. Write a check (✓) next to each of those that you do not know.

Some of these words and idioms may be completely new for you. Find them in the reading. Use the sentences around them to understand what they mean. Note how they are used. These are the words and idioms to learn for this story.

1. _____ an **acre** (noun): a measurement of land (2.5 acres = 1 hectare)

2. _____ an **adult** (noun): a person over the age of 18

3. _____ **autumn** (noun): the season of the year between summer and winter; fall; harvest time

4. _____ to **bolt** (verb): to run suddenly; to dash forward

5. _____ **brawn** (non-count noun): strength

6. _____ a **bucket** (noun): a container with a handle for carrying water or other things

7. _____ **burlap** (non-count noun): a type of strong, thick, coarse cloth made from hemp or jute

8. _____ a **canning factory** (noun): a place where food is saved and put into cans

9. _____ to **deduct** (verb): to subtract; to take away

10. _____ a **din** (noun): a loud and unpleasant sound

11. _____ to **earn** (verb): to work for money; to do a job and be paid for it

12. _____ to **feel welcome** (idiom): to understand that one can visit and know that people are glad to show it

13. _____ to **flap** (verb): to move like a bird's wing; to flutter

14. _____ a **flock** (noun): a number of birds or sheep as a group

15. _____ **grassy** (adjective): covered with grass (used to describe ground)

16. _____ a **hawk** (noun): a large bird that eats other birds and small animals

17. _____ a **herd** (noun): a number of animals, such as cows or horses, together as a group

18. _____ **high noon** (idiom): the hottest time of the day, between 12 and 2 p.m.

19. _____ the **hired help** (noun/idiom): the person or people who are paid to work on a farm

20. _____ a **hoof** (noun): the hard, split foot of a cow, horse, or sheep (plural = *hooves*)

21. _____ a **hullabaloo** (noun): a din; a lot of noise caused by people or animals

22. _____ an **insight** (noun): a sudden understanding of facts

23. _____ to **kneel** (verb): to go down on one's knees and settle there

24. _____ a **lung** (noun): one of two air-holding body organs

25. _____ a **meadow** (noun): a field of grass where animals can eat the grass

26. _____ **motivation** (non-count noun): a goal; a reason for doing something

27. _____ **obvious** (adjective): clearly understood

28. _____ a **pail** (noun): a bucket; a container for carrying water

29. _____ **planted** (adjective): unmoving; stable

30. _____ to **pluck** (verb): to pick; to pull off

31. _____ a **sack** (noun): a piece of cloth that is sewn so that it can hold goods; a paper that is folded and glued to hold items

32. _____ to **stretch out** (idiom): to lie down and prepare to rest or sleep

33. _____ **stubbornly** (adverb): firmly, without listening to reason

34. _____ to **surround** (verb): to be on all sides (with something in the middle)

35. _____ a **thunderstorm** (noun): a rainstorm with thunder and lightning

36. _____ a **whirring sound** (idiom): a soft sound of an engine or birds' wings moving

37. _____ a **yearling** (noun): an animal that is a year old; an adolescent animal

After You Have Read the Story

Do you have the answers to the questions from "While You Read the Story"? Talk about the answers with your classmates.

Understanding Sequence

A. In the blank in front of each sentence, write 2–8 to show that you know the order of the part of the story about picking beans.

     a. _____ We picked beans all morning and all afternoon.

     b. _____ Uncle John took the beans to the canning factory.

     c. __1__ We got up early and put on our bean-picking clothes.

d. _____ We chose a row of beans and began to pick them.

e. _____ Uncle John drove the truck back to town with us in the back.

f. _____ We made lunches to take with us, and we put them into paper sacks.

g. _____ Uncle John came to town to pick us up in his yellow truck.

h. _____ Our bags of beans were weighed, and we got three cents for every pound.

B. In the blank in front of each sentence, write 2–8 to show that you know the order of the part of the story about the turkeys.

a. _____ We woke up, and we could feel eyes on us.

b. _____ The day was too hot to be in the fields at noon, so we went to take a rest.

c. _____ There was a great hullabaloo.

d. __1__ We went to the farm to pick beans and earn some money.

e. _____ I made a whirring sound, and the turkeys settled down.

f. _____ My cousin and I found a cool place to rest.

g. _____ We escaped from the turkeys.

h. _____ Both of us fell asleep.

C. In the blank in front of each sentence, write 2–8 to show that you know the order of the part of the story about the yearling.

a. _____ The cows came peacefully to the barn.

b. _____ The yearling was afraid to go into the barn, so she wouldn't move.

c. _____ Ted asked if he could try.

d. _____ Ted pulled back on the yearling's tail.

e. __1__ A thunderstorm was coming.

f. _____ Uncle John and his son Dan tried to pull the yearling into the barn.

g. _____ The yearling ran straight into the barn.

h. _____ Ted and I went to the meadow to get the cows.

Answering Questions About the Story

Read these questions, think about the answers, and then discuss the answers with your classmates.

1. What time did Uncle John come to town to pick up the bean-pickers?
2. Why didn't he come earlier?
3. Why did the children wear light-colored shirts with long sleeves?
4. How much can a gunnysack hold?
5. What other use did they have for gunnysacks besides holding beans?
6. How much does a gunnysack weigh?
7. Who was Dan?
8. Why did Mrs. Miller go to pick beans?
9. How did Mrs. Miller help the storyteller?
10. Who was Peggy?

Drawing Conclusions from the Story

Which of these statements are probably true, from the information in the story? Write *true* or *false* in the blank in front of each sentence.

1. _____ Uncle John sold the beans for three cents a pound.
2. _____ Beans are ready to pick in July.
3. _____ Uncle John needed a lot of clean empty gunnysacks every day.
4. _____ An adult could earn between five and ten dollars a day working on a farm.

5. _____ Children are better workers than adults.

6. _____ The noon sun can be dangerous.

7. _____ Children like to play.

8. _____ A lot of noise can be frightening.

9. _____ Hawks eat turkeys.

10. _____ Some people can "feel" others looking at them.

11. _____ The turkeys settled into the grass to sleep when they heard the whirring sound.

12. _____ The sky gets light before a thunderstorm.

13. _____ It is dangerous for cows to be in a meadow during a bad thunderstorm.

14. _____ Horses don't ever go into a barn.

15. _____ All cows are stubborn.

Finding the Meaning in Context

Which meaning is closest to the underlined word or words? Circle *a, b, c,* or *d.*

1. I learned a lot about having <u>a goal</u> in life from picking beans on the farm.

   a. motivation   c. a good lunch

   b. common sense   d. another lesson

2. The gunnysacks weighed two pounds, so Uncle John <u>took off</u> two pounds from the weight of the full bags to weigh just the beans.

   a. figured out   c. deducted

   b. hired   d. stretched out

3. The turkeys were frightened by us when we woke up. They made a <u>lot of noise</u>.

   a. dark   c. day

   b. dairy   d. din

4. Each of us had a paper bag with a lunch and a <u>pail</u> to put our beans in.

   a. sack   c. hat

   b. bucket   d. shirt

5. The gunnysacks were made of <u>a thick coarse cloth</u>.

   a. paper   c. burlap

   b. hullabaloo   d. grass

6. The turkeys <u>were on all sides of</u> us.

   a. stretch out on   c. ran to

   b. bolted toward   d. surrounded

7. The horses were all in their <u>places in the barn</u>.

   a. barns   c. buildings

   b. meadows   d. stalls

8. The trees turn beautiful colors in the <u>fall</u>.

   a. autumn   c. barn

   b. herd   d. din

Matching New Words and Meanings

Draw a line between the two words or phrases with similar meanings.

   1. bucket   a. brawn

   2. hullabaloo   b. bag

   3. earn   c. hoof

   4. sack   d. pail

   5. pick   e. rest

   6. stretch out   f. din

   7. strong   g. calf

   8. foot   h. pay

   9. meadow   i. pluck

  10. yearling   j. field

Practicing with Idioms

Find the idiom or expression in the Words and Idioms List or from the story that means the same as the underlined word or words and write the correct form of it in the blank.

1. My cousin and I found a cool place under a tree. We <u>lay down</u> and went to sleep.

    My cousin and I found a cool place under a tree. We _____ and went to sleep.

2. Uncle John and <u>several men who worked for him</u> took the bags of beans to the canning factory in pick-up trucks.

    Uncle John and _____ took the bags of beans to the canning factory in pick-up trucks.

3. The air is hottest at <u>the time between twelve and two</u>.

    The air is hottest at _____ .

4. The wings of a hawk make a <u>sound like a small engine</u>.

    The wings of a hawk make a _____ .

5. Aunt Wanda always made us <u>glad that we had come to the farm to visit</u>.

    Aunt Wanda always made us _____ .

6. Uncle John weighed the bags of beans, and Aunt Wanda <u>determined</u> how much money we had earned.

    Uncle John weighed the bags of beans, and Aunt Wanda _____ how much money we had earned.

7. Ted watched the two men pulling on the stubborn yearling, and he used <u>his ability to think</u> to find a way to get the animal into the barn.

    Ted watched the two men pulling on the stubborn yearling, and he used _____ to find a way to get the animal into the barn.

8. Ted and I rode our bicycles to the farm <u>so that we could be there the whole day</u>.

Ted and I rode our bicycles to the farm _____ .

Exploring the Ideas

Think about these questions. Talk about your opinions with your classmates.

1. What motivates you?
2. How many pounds of beans did a person have to pick to earn $5? $7?
3. Why do some people earn more money than others?
4. Were the children hired help? Why or why not?
5. Why did John make two stops with his yellow truck in the morning?
6. Have you ever felt eyes looking at you? How did it feel? Did you like the feeling?
7. Why did Peggy start to cry?
8. Why do you think the yearling refused to go into the barn?
9. What did Ted see that Uncle John and Dan did not see?
10. Why is a barn safer than a meadow for animals during a thunderstorm?

Finding the Differences

What's the difference between...

1. a flock and a herd?
2. a lunch sack and a gunnysack?
3. a shady place and a grassy place?
4. a cow and a yearling?
5. autumn and fall?
6. a truck and a bicycle?
7. a bag and a sack?
8. a bucket and a pail?
9. a barn and a stall?
10. using one's brain and using one's brawn?

Making Inferences

Read the numbered sentence. Then read the sentences under it. Which ones are true because the numbered sentence is true? Circle the letter in front of each true statement.

1. Uncle John drove his yellow truck to town every morning and picked up the bean-pickers.

    a. Uncle John's truck was very small.

    b. Uncle John lived on the farm.

    c. All yellow trucks are good for carrying people.

    d. We children liked to ride in the back of the truck.

    e. The children needed a ride to the farm.

    f. It is always safe to ride in the back of a truck.

    g. Uncle John really needed help with picking the beans.

2. My brothers played, and they never got more than two dollars for the beans they picked.

    a. My brothers weren't good workers.

    b. My brothers didn't have good motivation to pick beans.

    c. There were lots of things to do that were fun on the farm.

    d. My brothers were younger than I was.

    e. The two boys didn't pick many beans.

3. When we woke up, we realized that a flock of 100 or more turkeys surrounded us.

    a. We hadn't seen the turkeys when we stretched out on the grass.

    b. The turkeys came while we were asleep.

    c. The turkeys were hot in the sun and wanted to be in the shade.

    d. We had fallen asleep.

    e. The turkeys always spent part of the afternoon under the tree.

    f. A hawk was following the turkeys.

    g. Turkeys stay together in a group.

    h. There weren't many turkeys.

4. It was obvious that there was going to be a thunderstorm.

    a. There were clouds in the sky.

    b. The cows were happy in the meadow.

    c. The sky was light, and the sun was shining.

    d. The wind began to blow.

    e. The sky grew dark.

    f. We knew the signs of a coming storm.

5. Uncle John and his son Dan didn't think Ted could get the yearling into the barn.

    a. Ted was young and not very strong.

    b. Uncle John and Dan were able to get the yearling into the barn.

    c. Ted didn't look strong enough to pull the yearling into the barn.

    d. Ted had a big rope.

    e. The two men considered Ted a smart child.

Finding the Main Ideas

There are three small stories in this story. Each one is a lesson that the storyteller learned. Arrange the ideas from these three stories into three columns on the next page.

1. It's better to think than to use force in solving a problem.

2. One should not work in the heat of the day.

3. It is good to watch what others do to learn a better way.

4. It is good to protect oneself from the sun.

5. Some things come naturally.

6. It is good to have a goal.

7. We are often afraid of unusual things that happen.

8. A person can be a good model for a young person to follow.

9. Common sense is not common.

Picking Beans	Talking to Turkeys	Getting the Yearling into the Barn

Reading for Details

Find the answers to these questions in the story.

1. How many pounds of beans can a gunnysack hold?
2. How much did Mrs. Miller pick in one day?
3. How did the children protect themselves from the sun?
4. How many turkeys surrounded the storyteller and Peggy?
5. What bird do turkeys fear?
6. What sound do turkeys make?
7. Where do cows spend the day?
8. How much did Uncle John pay for each pound of beans that the pickers picked?

Taking a Close Look at the Meanings of the Words

1. The word *motivation* has the word *motive* and the word *move* in it. Therefore, *motivation* gives a person a reason or a motive for doing something. To do an action, a person must *move*.

2. The word *hullabaloo* sounds like the noise of many people. There is another word that is similar: *hubbub*. A *hullabaloo* is confusion; however, a *hubbub* can mean the sound of a lot of people who are busy. *Hubbub* is a positive word, and *hullabaloo* is not.

3. The *whir* of an engine is a soft sound. Try to make that sound. Your tongue must move from the air that you force out of your lungs. What are some other things that whir?

4. Hawks have very good eyesight. An expression in English about someone with sharp eyesight is to say that the person has *eyes like a hawk*. Hawks can see tiny animals in fields. They eat mice, for example. Why do you think turkeys are afraid of them?

A Perfect Job

The house seemed too large, too much for a young person to clean—especially the long porches with many windows!

Before You Read the Story

Use these questions as preparation for reading the story. If you need to know the meaning of a word or idiom, check the Words and Idioms List after the story.

1. What does the title mean to you?
2. What are some things that are perfect?
3. Did the storyteller like the job?
4. What were the storyteller's favorite parts of the day? Why?

While You Read the Story

Read these questions and look for the answers as you read the story.

1. Why did Granny sometimes give the storyteller one dollar and sometimes three or four dollars?
2. What did Granny always give the storyteller at the end of the day (besides some money)?
3. What was Granny trying to teach her grandchild?
4. What did the storyteller learn?

A Perfect Job

1   My job was to help Granny. Every Saturday morning, usually about ten o'clock, I rode my bicycle the mile to her house. I knocked on her door and waited. She opened the door, and I went in. First I had a little breakfast

5   with her, usually sweet cinnamon rolls and milk. She always asked about my mother and father and brothers and sisters. Then the work started. I went to the basement and got out the broom, the mop, the bucket, and clean rags.

10   Granny had a big closet full of cleaning supplies. My job was to clean her big house. It would usually take me two or three hours. I could hear Granny going out and about. She was always a busy woman.

Granny liked it when I started upstairs. So I always started

15   with the three bedrooms. With her big powerful vacuum cleaner, I swept the big rugs. Next I used a string mop with a nice-smelling oil on it to clean the wood floors. With a damp rag and some mild soap, I wiped the window sills. I changed the sheets on her bed too. She slept in a small room, and it was

20   easy to clean that room. I used the mop to get dust from under her bed. Sometimes I found socks and slippers under there too.

Another job upstairs was to clean the bathroom. I used a cleaning powder on the bathtub and a wash basin and a brush on the toilet. I washed the linoleum floor with pine-scented

25   water. That made the bathroom smell clean and fresh. I had to empty the wastebaskets and carry the trash outside. I also had to take the bathroom rug downstairs to be washed in the big old washing machine. I put a fresh one from the closet on the clean floor.

30   On the main floor of the house, there were two rooms. The kitchen was large and airy. There were big windows, and Granny kept it very clean. However, my job was to wipe the surface of everything—the stove, the cupboards, the table, and the chairs. She wanted her kitchen to sparkle. I had to

35 use clean cloths and change the water many times. Granny loved a clean kitchen. There was a pantry off the kitchen. It was filled with lots of cans of

40 food and bags of vegetables, like potatoes. Granny put a lot of stuff into that pantry. I had to clean it every week. I didn't

45 like that pantry very much.

    The living room and dining room were one big room with an arch between them. I vacuumed the rugs every week. I took the soft dust cloth and wiped the week's accumulation of dust from the piano, the china closet, the bookcases, and

50 the little tables. Sometimes I even shook out the beautiful Persian shawl on the piano.

    The last job was to sweep the porches. There was one on the front of the house and one on the back. I really didn't like those porches because sometimes I would see spiders, and I

55 was afraid of spiders. Sometimes I skipped the porches. I would fluff up the cushions and sweep just the doorways.

    Every week, when I had finished, Granny would give me something from her little blue money purse. First we would walk through her house, and she would note the things I

60 had done well. I remember that one day she noticed the clean mirrors. I had polished them that day. Another day

she noticed that I HAD really swept the porches. Some days she would say, "Not bad." And she would give me a dollar. Once in a while, she would say, "Good enough," and she would give me two dollars. One day, she gave me four dollars. It was the day I washed the windows with ammonia water and newspapers. She said, "Today you did a pretty good job."

I was suddenly interested. I asked, "Granny, what is a perfect job worth?"

"A perfect job?" she asked. "A perfect job is worth ten dollars." And she went to her big old refrigerator for the chocolate milk. She knew that I loved chocolate milk. There was always a glass of chocolate milk for me at the end of my work on Saturday.

The next Saturday I got up at seven in the morning. I was at Granny's house before eight o'clock. I took furniture polish, floor oil, and ammonia upstairs with me. And I began to work fast. I washed the windows and the mirrors. I opened a window and shook out the small rugs. I vacuumed and polished. I dusted and wiped. I washed the floor in the bathroom twice. Then I put some polish on it, and it shone. After I emptied the trash, I even washed out the wastebaskets. I could hear Granny, coming in and going out, downstairs.

In the kitchen I scrubbed the floor. I cleaned the stove, inside and out. Granny had gone to the store, so I took the silverware out of the drawers and washed out the drawers. I took everything out of the pantry. I scrubbed the shelves and washed that floor really well. When the shelves were dry, I straightened the cans on the shelves too. I arranged the pots and pans, and I scrubbed the kitchen sink. I even scrubbed the area under the kitchen sink.

Next I attacked the living room with great energy. I took the cushions from the sofa outside and beat them. Clouds of dust rose from them. I used an attachment on the vacuum
95 cleaner to get them really clean. I polished the piano with furniture polish. Then I did the same for the dining table and the chairs. I even polished the legs of the table. I straightened the books on the shelves of the bookcases. Then I made the
100 porches shine, and I washed the windows there too. It was past five o'clock when I finished. The house smelled clean, and it looked clean too.

I found Granny outside. She was looking at her flowers. "I'm finished, Granny," I said. I really needed the chocolate
105 milk. She stopped in the kitchen, opened the refrigerator, and took out the milk. She put a plate of my favorite cookies on the table too. "Let's walk through the house first," she said with a smile.

I knew that she was pleased. She smiled when she
110 looked into the bathroom. "It shines," she said. She noted that I had dusted everything in the bedroom, even the bottles on the bureau. She commented on the bathroom floor and the floors of the porches. She stopped to play a few notes on the piano. She looked under the dining room table. She could
115 see how clean everything was. "Child," she said, "today you have done a perfect job."

Words and Idioms List

You already know some of these words and idioms. Go through the list. Write a check (✓) next to each of those that you do not know.

Some of these words and idioms may be completely new for you. Find them in the reading. Use the sentences around them to understand what they mean. Note how they are used. These are the words and idioms to learn for this story.

1. _____ an **accumulation** (noun): an increase of something over time

2. _____ **airy** (adjective): full of air; with good ventilation

3. _____ **ammonia** (non-count noun): NH_4; a bad-smelling cleaning liquid that dissolves grease

4. _____ an **arch** (noun): a curved doorway, usually without a door

5. _____ an **attachment** (noun): an extra piece (here, a hose to clean furniture that is attached or connected to a vacuum cleaner)

6. _____ to **attack** (verb): to fight against (here, to begin to work with great energy and enthusiasm)

7. _____ a **bureau** (noun): a large piece of furniture that is used to store clothing in drawers

8. _____ a **china closet** (noun): a large piece of furniture, usually with fancy glass doors, in which dishes and glasses are kept

9. _____ **cinnamon** (non-count noun): a spice used in making sweet breads and rolls

10. _____ to **comment on** (verb): to give an opinion about

11. _____ a **cushion** (noun): a hard pillow (Usually a sofa or couch has cushions on it.)

12. _____ **damp** (adjective): slightly wet

13. _____ a **drawer** (noun): a box with handles that is pulled out of a desk or bureau, used for storing things

14. _____ **dust** (non-count noun): tiny particles in the air that collect on the top of furniture

15. _____ to **fluff up** (verb): to cause to become large by adding air to the inside of

16. _____ **linoleum** (non-count noun): a rubber or plastic floor covering that can be colored or patterned, used for kitchen floors

17. _____ a **mop** (noun): a cleaning tool on a stick, used to wash or remove dust from floors

18. _____ a **pantry** (noun): a small room for storage of kitchen things and food

19. _____ **perfect** (adjective): not having any weak points or mistakes

20. _____ to **play a few notes** (idiom): to try to play a musical instrument

21. _____ to **polish something** (verb): to use an oil or other liquid to make something like furniture shine

22. _____ a **porch** (noun): a long room, usually not heated in winter, on the front or back of a house (Some porches have windows and screens; others are open.)

23. _____ **pots and pans** (plural nouns as an idiom): metal containers in which foods are cooked

24. _____ **rags** (plural noun): pieces of cloth used for cleaning

25. _____ to **scrub** (verb): to clean with a brush

26. _____ to **shake out** (verb): to hold onto one edge of (a cloth or rug) and move it up and down to remove dust and dirt

27. _____ a **shawl** (noun): a triangle of cloth, used to keep one's shoulders warm

28. _____ a **sheet** (noun): a large cotton piece of cloth put over a bed to protect the mattress and the area under the blankets

29. _____ to **shine** (verb): to reflect light (past tense = *shone*)

30. _____ **silverware** (non-count noun): knives, forks, and spoons used for eating and serving food

31. _____ to **sparkle** (verb): to shine because of being clean

32. _____ a **spider** (noun): an eight-legged insect that makes webs

33. _____ to **straighten** (verb): to put into order

34. _____ to **sweep** (verb): to clean dirt from a floor with a broom

35. _____ **trash** (non-count noun): garbage; things to throw away

36. _____ to **vacuum** (verb): to clean with an electric machine that sucks in air and dust

37. _____ a **wash basin** (noun): a bathroom sink with a faucet and a drain for water to escape

38. _____ a **window sill** (noun): a piece of wood at the bottom of a window frame

39. _____ to **wipe** (verb): to use a cloth to clean the surface of

After You Have Read the Story

Do you have the answers to the questions from "While You Read the Story"? Talk about the questions with your classmates.

Understanding Sequence

In the blank in front of each sentence, write 2–8 to show that you know the order of the story.

a. _____ I had a glass of chocolate milk and went home.

b. _____ I rode my bicycle to Granny's house.

c. _____ Granny and I had a little breakfast together.

d. _____ It was necessary to clean the porches.

e. _____ I started cleaning upstairs.

f. __1__ On a Saturday morning I woke up early to go to Granny's house.

g. _____ I cleaned the kitchen and the pantry.

h. _____ The living room and dining room were next.

Answering Questions About the Story

Read these questions, think about the answers, and then discuss the answers with your classmates.

1. How did the storyteller get to Granny's house?
2. Why did Granny need help on Saturdays?
3. How was the oil put on the wood floors?
4. Where are things kept in a kitchen?
5. Where was the washing machine?
6. What did Granny always notice?
7. How did Granny show that she was happy with the cleaning job?
8. What is in a silverware drawer?
9. What cleaning supplies did the storyteller use?
10. What did the storyteller use rags for?

Drawing Conclusions from the Story

Which of these statements are probably true, from the information in the story? Write *true* or *false* in the blank in front of each sentence.

1. _____ Granny loved her grandchild.
2. _____ Granny wanted to help her grandchild learn to be a good worker.
3. _____ Granny didn't like to work.
4. _____ Granny spent a lot of time in her bedroom.
5. _____ Granny spent a lot of time in her pantry.
6. _____ Granny spent a lot of time in her kitchen.
7. _____ Granny played the piano.

8. _____ Granny never read books.

9. _____ Granny likes chocolate milk.

10. _____ Granny knew what her grandchild liked to eat.

Finding the Meaning in Context

Which meaning is closest to the underlined word or words? Circle *a, b, c,* or *d.*

1. There were three thick <u>pillows</u> on the sofa.
   a. chairs
   b. cloths
   c. rags
   d. cushions

2. Granny kept her things for cooking in her <u>pantry</u>.
   a. drawer
   b. bureau
   c. kitchen closet
   d. china closet

3. Granny kept her <u>things for cooking</u> in in her kitchen.
   a. pots and pans
   b. silverware
   c. dishes and glasses
   d. cleaning supplies

4. Granny wanted her kitchen to <u>sparkle</u>.
   a. wipe
   b. shine
   c. scrub
   d. polish

5. I <u>washed</u> the floor <u>with a brush</u> and pine-scented water.
   a. damp
   b. wiped
   c. straightened
   d. scrubbed

6. There was dust on the <u>lower part of the window frame</u>.
   a. window
   b. window sill
   c. mirror
   d. window top

7. I <u>didn't clean</u> the stove.
   a. wiped
   b. skipped
   c. scrubbed
   d. polished

8. I washed and polished all the <u>knives, forks, and spoons</u>.
   a. china
   b. silverware
   c. pots and pans
   d. rags

9. Everything in the kitchen <u>sparkled</u>.
   a. shone
   b. cleaned
   c. wiped
   d. airy

10. A porch is always <u>airy</u>.
    a. light and open
    b. damp
    c. like a kitchen
    d. dusty

Matching New Words and Meanings

Draw a line between the two words or phrases with similar meanings.

1. cookie	a. vacuum
2. polish	b. shine
3. wash	c. cinnamon roll
4. sparkle	d. slipper
5. bureau	e. scrub
6. wash basin	f. china closet
7. sweep	g. chair
8. sock	h. wipe
9. broom	i. mop
10. sofa	j. sink

Finding the Differences

What's the difference between …

1. a broom and a mop?
2. a broom and a vacuum cleaner?
3. a sink and a wash basin?
4. a closet and a pantry?
5. a cupboard and a china closet?

6. cans of food and bags of food?

7. a mirror and a window?

8. a refrigerator and a stove?

9. furniture polish and ammonia water?

10. a glass and a plate?

11. a sofa and a cushion?

12. a room and a porch?

13. a rug and a shawl?

14. a can and a bottle?

15. ammonia water and pine-scented water?

Practicing with Idioms

Find the idiom in the Words and Idioms List that means the same or almost the same as the underlined word or words and write the correct form of it in the blank.

1. Granny stopped at the piano and <u>made some music on it</u>.

   Granny stopped at the piano and _____ .

2. I began to clean the bathroom <u>with great energy</u>.

   I _____ the bathroom.

3. I needed to <u>remove the dust from</u> the small rugs, so I opened the window and did it.

   I needed _____ the small rugs, so I opened the window and did it.

4. Granny often <u>said something about</u> how clean the mirrors or the windows were.

   Granny often _____ how clean the mirrors or the windows were.

5. If there was a job that I didn't like, I sometimes <u>didn't do</u> it.

   If there was a job that I didn't like, I sometimes _____ it.

6. In the pantry I <u>put</u> all the cans <u>in order</u>.

   In the pantry I _____ all the cans.

7. I washed all the dishes that were in the <u>piece of furniture that holds dishes and glasses</u>.

   I washed all the dishes that were in the _____ .

8. I used <u>a special extra piece</u> for the vacuum cleaner to take the dust from the sofa cushions.

   I used _____ for the vacuum cleaner to take the dust from the sofa cushions.

Exploring the Ideas

Think about these questions. Talk about your opinions with your classmates.

1. Did Granny really need to have the storyteller come to help her?
2. How did Granny teach the storyteller about doing a really good job?
3. What made the job a perfect job?
4. How did Granny know that the storyteller was doing a really good job?
5. Why did the storyteller have to go to the basement?

Making Inferences

A. Answer these questions.

1. What things does a clean house smell like?
2. How do we know that Granny liked music?
3. Why was it necessary for the storyteller to help Granny with the cleaning?
4. Do you think the storyteller was a good worker?
5. Why did the storyteller get up early one Saturday morning?

B. Read the numbered sentence. Then read the sentences under it. Which ones are true because the numbered sentence is true? Circle the letter in front of each true statement.

1. Granny was always a busy woman.

   a. Granny didn't like to clean.

   b. Granny had lots of things to do.

   c. Granny had lots of energy.

   d. Granny enjoyed being busy.

2. Granny had a big house.

   a. It took two hours to clean her house.

   b. There was an upstairs and a basement.

   c. There were three bedrooms to clean.

   d. There was a big kitchen.

3. Granny had a big closet full of cleaning supplies.

   a. Granny cleaned her house every day.

   b. Granny wanted to have everything ready for the storyteller to do a really good job.

   c. Granny had a lot of old bottles.

   d. Granny should have thrown away many of the old cleaning supplies.

   e. Granny did a lot of cleaning herself.

4. Granny had a lot of cans of food in her pantry.

   a. She didn't cook much.

   b. She liked to have food on hand.

   c. She didn't want to go shopping very often.

   d. She ate a lot.

5. Granny always had a little breakfast ready.

   a. She loved her grandchild.

   b. She liked to eat breakfast with someone else.

   c. It was a good way to start the day.

   d. It made the storyteller happy.

Finding the Main Ideas

Which title or titles will be appropriate for this story? Circle the letter in front of each one.

    a. Every Saturday Morning

    b. Helping Granny

    c. Earning Ten Dollars

    d. Washing Windows

    e. A Day in the Pantry

    f. Spiders on the Porch

    g. Doing a Perfect Job of Cleaning

    h. A Working Day

Reading for Details

Find the answers to these questions in the story.

1. Where were the cleaning supplies in Granny's house?
2. At what time did the storyteller usually start?
3. What did Granny have on her floors?
4. What are sheets on a bed?
5. How much time did the cleaning job usually take?
6. What day was the day to help Granny?
7. What did the storyteller use to clean the toilet?
8. What did the storyteller use ammonia water and newspapers to clean?
9. Where were there spiders in the house?
10. What is the little room off the kitchen called?
11. What was in the little room off the kitchen?
12. Where was the Persian shawl?

Taking a Close Look at the Meanings of the Words

1. Note that a *brush* is used *to brush* or *to scrub*. A mop is used to *mop a floor*. A *broom* is used to *sweep a floor*. A *vacuum cleaner* is used to *sweep a rug*. *To dust* is to *remove dust*, and one uses a cloth or a rag to dust. One can use a liquid *polish* to *polish* furniture or a floor. Polishing makes something shine.

2. The words *trash, waste,* and *garbage* all mean things that we throw away. In different communities, different meanings (or slightly different meanings) are attached to each word.

3. *Cloth* is a plain piece of material, usually cotton. A *rag* is a piece of cloth that is old, probably from old clothing.

4. *Ammonia* is a strong chemical. You can buy it at the store. A half a cup of ammonia in a pail of water is a strong cleaner. Ammonia is a poison. It can burn the eyes and the skin. Even the smell is bad for a person. Use ammonia water only when there is lots of fresh air. Never mix ammonia with any other cleaning chemical.

5. The name *Granny* is one of the common names for *grandmother*. Others are *Grandma, Nana, Gramma, Grams,* and *Grandmum*.

The Day Anna Kadulski Learned to Drive

Anna and her three children had to carry on after Frank died. Carrying on meant continuing, accepting the challenges—even the job of driving the car!

Before You Read the Story

Use these questions as preparation for reading the story. If you need to know the meaning of a word or idiom, check the Words and Idioms List after the story.

1. How many words do you know about the topic of driving? Make a list of these words with your classmates.

2. Think about the title of this story. What will it be about? Circle the ideas and words that you expect to find in a story with this title.

car	tires	police	driving	learning
fire	food	school	lessons	gasoline
sell	books	bridge	chicken	grocery store
buy	health	shopping		

While You Read the Story

Read these questions and look for the answers as you read the story.

1. What is your opinion about Anna Kadulski and her learning to drive? Do you think it was easy for her?

2. Who tells the story?

3. How would Anna have told the story?

The Day Anna Kadulski Learned to Drive

1   When my dad died on January 5 in 1925, he left a lot behind. He left a widow, three young children, a thriving grocery store business, and a new black Franklin in the garage.

5   The Franklin was the only one in town, and it was special. I remember the big shiny dome of a hood on that car. I also remember that no one in our tiny hometown really knew how to take care of it, except my dad. And Frank Kadulski was gone.

10   In those days, the men gathered at our Standard Oil station. My dad had said one day, out of the blue, "They'll need gasoline fuel for cars!" The next thing we knew, he had built a gas station. He added it to the little complex of grain warehouse, smokehouse, ice barn, horse barn, chicken yard, 15 and grocery store.

My dad was a very good businessman. He understood supply and demand. Our Standard Oil station was the first one in town. And the men gathered there. Men who had cars came to buy gas. Men without cars came to learn about 20 them. Those men at the Standard Oil station used to say that my dad should have bought a Ford. To fix a Ford, they said, all you needed was a piece of haywire.

25   Now Dad was gone, and that big and fancy Franklin sat. My mother didn't know how to drive it. She didn't know how to drive anything. She probably wouldn't have driven it even if she had known how.

30   I think that maybe my mother was afraid of that automobile. When she wanted to go somewhere, she had to find a driver. And a lot of the Polish men she trusted to drive her anywhere were also afraid of—well, respectful of—that grand Franklin.

     Uncle John, her younger brother, was not afraid. He wasn't 35 afraid of my mother. He wasn't afraid of new things. He wasn't afraid of anything, not even that Franklin. He wasn't even afraid of teaching his sister how to drive. One hot and dry Sunday afternoon, Uncle John and Aunt Wanda came to our house in their spotless black Ford. I remember that he 40 parked it in our backyard. My sister, my brother, and I came out to welcome them. Then Uncle John told us all to get into the Franklin. We did—my mother, my sister, my brother,

Aunt Wanda, Uncle John, and I. My mother sat in the front seat with her brother. We were off for 45 a Sunday afternoon ride.

     We went out of town, down the familiar dusty roads to Uncle John's farm. He had a farm along the river, less than twenty minutes 50 or two and a half miles from the limits of town. When we got to the farmhouse, Uncle John stopped. Aunt Wanda got out, and we started to follow her. Uncle John told us to stay put. Then 55 he drove through the farmyard and out into a big field.

     He stopped and got out of the driver's seat. "Anna," he said, "it's your turn!" At first she was speechless. Then she refused, she pleaded, she almost cried, but then she laughed. "You can't hurt anything but your pride out here," he said.

60   She got out of the passenger seat, went around to the front of the car, and got the car engine started. My mother was a powerful woman. She was used to hard work, but she knew nothing about cars. Then she got in and started driving. It wasn't smooth at first. Her brother explained one thing
65   and then another. We three children understood nothing. We couldn't see much over the front seats of the car anyway. There were some bumps and grinding sounds from the motor, and some shrieks, too. Maybe those sounds were scared chickens or field rocks and bushes under the car. In
70   any case, we were careful not to laugh out loud. But two hours later, my mother was driving! Her face was all smiles. She looked very pleased with herself. And Uncle John looked proud. My sister, my brother, and I had a great time.

       We sat in the back seat for forty minutes more, and our
75   mother drove us all the way home.

Words and Idioms List

You already know some of these words and idioms. Go through the list. Write a check (✓) next to each of those that you do not know.

Some of these words and idioms may be completely new for you. Find them in the reading. Use the sentences around them to understand what they mean. Note how they are used. These are the words and idioms to learn for this story.

1. _____ to **be all smiles** (idiom): to be very happy about something

2. _____ to **be speechless** (idiom): to be too surprised to speak

3. _____ a **bump** (noun): a sound or feeling of one thing hitting another

4. _____ a **complex** (noun): a group of related buildings (perhaps owned by one person)

5. _____ a **dome** (noun): a smooth, curved shape (like the top half of a ball)

6. _____ a **grinding sound** (idiom): the sound of a motor that isn't running smoothly

7. _____ the **hood** (noun): the metal cover over a car engine

8. _____ to **leave something behind** (idiom): to give as a gift after one's death (said of a person who has died); to forget to take something (said of a person who is living)

9. _____ **out of the blue** (idiom): without any warning

10. _____ the **passenger seat** (noun): the seat next to the driver (in a car or truck)

11. _____ to **plead** (verb): to beg; to ask for something, with sincere feelings

12. _____ **shiny** (adjective): bright and smooth

13. _____ **spotless** (adjective): perfectly clean

14. _____ to **stay put** (idiom): not to move

15. _____ to **take care of something** (idiom): to know how to manage something

16. _____ **thriving** (adjective): growing; healthy

17. _____ to **understand supply and demand** (idiom): to realize that one person can make money by providing what others want to buy

18. _____ a **widow** (noun): a woman whose husband has died

After You Have Read the Story

Do you have the answers to the questions from "While You Read the Story"? Talk about the answers with your classmates.

Understanding Sequence

In the blank in front of each sentence, write 2–10 to show that you know the order of the story.

a. _____ Anna Kadulski drove home very slowly.

b. _____ Uncle John and Aunt Wanda came to the house and parked in the backyard.

c. ___1__ Frank Kadulski bought a fine new Franklin.

d. _____ We got into the car, and Uncle John drove us to his farm.

e. _____ We heard bumps, shrieks, and grinding sounds.

f. _____ Frank Kadulski died.

g. _____ Aunt Wanda got out of the car at the farmhouse, but we had to stay put.

h. _____ Anna Kadulski had to ask other people to drive her from place to place in her car.

i. _____ Anna practiced driving in a field until she could do it.

j. _____ Uncle John taught Anna how to drive.

Answering Questions About the Story

Read these questions, think about the answers, and then discuss the answers with your classmates.

1. What do Fords and Franklins have in common?
2. What did they sell at the Standard Oil station?
3. Who was Uncle John married to?
4. What was necessary to fix a Ford, according to the men at the Standard Oil station?
5. Where did Uncle John live?

6. What was special about the Franklin?

7. Name the parts of Frank Kadulski's business complex.

8. Where did Anna learn how to drive?

9. Where was Uncle John's farm?

10. How fast did Anna drive home?

Drawing Conclusions from the Reading

Answer these questions with your own ideas.

1. What kind of person was Uncle John?

2. How was Anna a powerful woman?

3. Why couldn't her children see what was happening during the driving lesson?

4. How did the gasoline station show that Frank Kadulski understood supply and demand?

5. Why were the three children in the back seat?

6. Why did Uncle John choose a field for the driving lesson?

7. Why was Anna Kadulski speechless?

8. What made Uncle John proud?

9. Do we know Uncle John's last name? Why or why not?

10. How did a driver start the engine of a Franklin?

11. Which is simpler, a Ford or a Franklin? How do you know?

12. Why was a spotless car unusual in those days?

Finding the Meaning in Context

Find the word in this list that means the same or almost the same as the underlined word or words and write it in the blank.

warehouse	fuel	thriving	garage	familiar
respectful	grain	refused	spotless	gathered
powerful	shiny	widow		

1. John asked Wanda to dance, but she <u>said that she would not dance</u>.

John asked Wanda to dance, but she _____ .

2. All the young people <u>met</u> at the swimming pool on hot summer days.

   All the young people _____ at the swimming pool on hot summer days.

3. To make a campfire, you need <u>something to burn</u>.

   To make a campfire, you need _____ .

4. Anna's house was always <u>perfectly clean</u>.

   Anna's house was always _____ .

5. Frank Kadulski had a <u>growing and profitable</u> business.

   Frank Kadulski had a _____ business.

6. They kept all the food in a large <u>building especially for storing things</u>.

   They kept all the food in a large _____ .

7. Anna's two daughters grew up to be <u>strong</u> women like their mother.

   Anna's two daughters grew up to be _____ women like their mother.

8. The farmer planted <u>wheat and corn</u> crops.

   The farmer planted _____ crops.

9. They kept the Franklin in a large <u>building for cars</u>.

   They kept the Franklin in a large _____ .

10. When the man died, his <u>wife</u> moved to another city.

    When the man died, his _____ moved to another city.

11. Although I have never been to this small town before this visit, everything here seems <u>comfortable and well-known</u> to me.

    Although I have never been to this small town before this visit,

    everything here seems _____ to me.

12. The children in the school were <u>polite</u> toward their teacher.

    The children in the school were _____ toward their teacher.

13. The children brought the teacher a big <u>bright and smooth</u> apple on the first day of school.

    The children brought the teacher a big _____ apple on the first day of school.

14. When John told her to start driving, she was <u>unable to say anything</u>.

    When John told her to start driving, she was _____ .

Finding Definitions for New Words

Draw a line between the word or phrase and its definition.

1.	pride	a.	land behind a house
2.	barn	b.	open area on a farm
3.	hood	c.	frightened
4.	smokehouse	d.	place where the first houses of a city are
5.	backyard	e.	feeling of self-respect
6.	limits of town	f.	farm building
7.	field	g.	rubbing; friction
8.	scared	h.	result of being hit by something
9.	bump	i.	place where meat is put to be treated
10.	grinding	j.	metal part of the top front section of a car

Finding the Differences

What's the difference between...

1. a backyard and a farmyard?
2. a wife and a widow?
3. a motor and an engine?
4. a Ford and a Franklin?
5. an aunt and an uncle?
6. a barn and a garage?

Matching New Words and Meanings

Draw a line between the two words with similar meanings.

1. engine   a. spotless
2. afraid   b. grand
3. automobile   c. motor
4. clean   d. scared
5. fancy   e. car

Practicing with Idioms

Find the idiom in this list that completes each sentence and write the correct form of it in the blank. Note that some words (for example, *[something]*) can be replaced with other words and might be in another position in the sentence. You can use some of them more than once.

to be all smiles	to get [something] started
to stay put	to understand supply and demand
to get out	to leave [something] behind
to be speechless	to take care of [something]

1. There was a fire at a farm outside of town, so everyone went to help put it out. My father took us with him, but we had to remain in the car. He told us to _____ .

2. The car door opened, and a lovely woman _____ .

3. When my sister tried on her wedding dress, I looked at her face and knew that she liked it. She was quiet, and she _____ .

4. When my father saw the whole family together for his birthday, he _____ . We were all surprised, because he always liked to talk.

5. The little girl put all her toy animals on a shelf. As she left, she turned and said to them, "Now you all _____ . I want to see you just like this when I come back."

6. The wood was too wet to burn easily, but the man used some newspaper and some gasoline on it to _____ .

7. A person who _____ will make money because he or she will be ready to sell what others want to buy.

8. When John Doe died, he _____ a lot of money for his children and grandchildren.

9. On Mother's Day, I sent flowers to my mother. When I saw her, she was pleased. She _____ .

10. The family went on a vacation, but their dog didn't go. They _____ .

11. Frank Kadulski was a good businessman. He _____ .

12. In our family, some of us work inside the house, and others _____ the yard and the garden.

Exploring the Ideas

Think about these questions. Talk about your opinions with your classmates.

1. A dome is a shape, like the top half of a ball. What are the names of four other shapes?

   _____ _____ _____ _____

   Name two things that have each of these shapes.

2. A hood is a part of a car. It protects the motor. What are some other parts of a car? What is the purpose of each of these other car parts?

3. What are some things about your home that are familiar to you?

4. Have you ever been speechless? When? Why?

Making Inferences

Which of these sentences are probably true? Circle the number in front of each one.

1. Anna Kadulski never drove very fast.
2. Her children were frightened because of the driving lesson.
3. Anna took her children with her wherever she went.
4. Anna's husband wanted her to learn how to drive.
5. It is good to have a car if you don't know how to drive.
6. Frank Kadulski was a good businessman because he had a big car.
7. A good businessman sees opportunities for business.
8. A good place to learn how to drive is a field on a farm.

Taking a Close Look at the Meanings of the Words

1. *To grind corn* is to put it between two stones and turn it into a powder of cornmeal. The stones make a sound, *a grinding sound*.
2. *To plead* is to ask for something, with great feeling. A *plea* is a sincere request.
3. The word *complex* can be a noun or an adjective. As a noun, a COMplex, the accent is on the first syllable. As an adjective, comPLEX, the accent is on the second syllable.

Katy Archer

The smiling face of Katy Archer tells the story of a woman of courage, line by line.

Before You Read the Story

Use these questions as preparation for reading the story. If you need to know the meaning of a word or idiom, check the Words and Idioms List after the story.

1. A story about a person's life is a biography. Why is this story likely to be a biography? Why do you think so?

2. What is a biography probably going to be like? How will it start?

3. Look at the pictures. What do the pictures tell you about Katy?

While You Read the Story

Read these questions and look for the answers as you read the story.

1. What difficulty did Katy have in life?

2. What were her dreams? What did she want to do in her life?

3. How much has Katy done (of what she intended to do)?

4. How is Katy a strong person? What parts of her life needed a lot of strength?

Katy Archer

1   Katy Archer is a senior citizen, and she is living life to the fullest. She wears her life on her wrinkled, smiling face.

"I choose to be what my mother was not," she says. "My mother was never happy."

Katy tells her story from the beginning. She was born in
5   Pocahontas, Illinois, in July of 1923. Her family lived on a farm. They were self-sufficient people because they grew all their own food. Their garden was full of all kinds of vegetables. They grew lettuce, beans,
10   asparagus, carrots, melons, and even popcorn. They had dairy cows too, and they sold milk and earned a dollar a day for the milk. They even had a horse and wagon for trips to town. However, Katy
15   was an imperfect child because she was born with a hearing impairment. She  was punished because she wouldn't listen. Her parents didn't know that she couldn't listen.

Katy did go to school, however. After she finished high
20   school, she wanted to be a nurse. She enrolled in a small nursing school, but she had to leave because of her hearing problem. Undaunted, Katy went to her family doctor, the same doctor who had delivered her. He helped her find a nursing school. She graduated in 1944. Katy and her friend
25   Betty tried to enlist in the Navy as nurses. Katy's friend was accepted, and Betty went off to the Great Lakes Naval Base in northern Illinois for training. Katy's friend was "off to see the world." Katy couldn't go because of her hearing.

Betty didn't see much of the world. She spent the next
30 five years at Great Lakes. That same year, however, Katy joined
the Army as a nurse and went to Europe. Wounded soldiers
came into the hospital 200 at a time. Katy worked with every
patient she had. She loved the work, and she stayed in
Europe for 20 months.

35 However, living conditions were hard. Katy got sick in the
harsh winter of wartime Europe, so she was transferred to the
Southwest, where the air is dry.

She was working at a veterans' hospital when she met her
husband, Joe. He was a patient, a wounded soldier. A year

40 after he left the hospital, he
and Katy got married. Both
of them wanted children, and
the children came fast. In nine
years they had four sons and
45 three daughters. Katy worked
at night so she could be at
home with her babies during
the day.

Katy's husband was not a
50 strong man psychologically.
He was often sad, and he
began to drink a lot. Then he
became very depressed. The man and wife never discussed
anything. They never argued, never fought. Joe would simply
55 walk out if a disagreement seemed to be arising. Joe was a
charming and talented man, but he could not share his talents
with his family. Katy realized that the children were hers, and
the problems were hers.

One day, Joe came home with two pieces of paper. They
were papers from a lawyer. "These are quit claims," he said.
"If something happens to one of us, the other gets everything."
Joe signed one of the papers. Katy signed hers, and Joe took
the papers away.

In 1973 Katy had a realization. She needed to get out of
the situation. Her seven children were all on their own.
However, Katy was very unhappy. Joe was drinking every
day. One day her parish priest asked her to stop to talk with
him. He told her that God did not intend her to be so
unhappy. She began to think about her situation. "My mother
was always unhappy. I didn't want to be."

She called their lawyer to find out about dividing their
property. She was told that all the property belonged to Joe.
He had filed a legal paper in which she had given up all
rights to their property. He had delivered the quit claim she
had signed, but not the one he was supposed to sign. Katy
had nothing of her own. She tried to talk to Joe, but he
walked out of the house.

It was Thanksgiving Day that she made the big decision.
Katy, as always, had made a big Thanksgiving dinner. She set
the table with her best dishes. She put the turkey, mashed
potatoes, gravy, and cranberries on her best tablecloth. She
called Joe to come to eat. He took a plate, filled it up, and
went to sit in front of the television set. He said nothing to
her. That day, Katy packed the first of three suitcases of
clothing and personal items. She hid it on the porch. Three
days later, she walked through the house. She said goodbye
to all her things. She stopped to pick up her mail. Then, with
her photograph albums and three bags, she got into the older
of the two family cars and drove away. She did not look back.

90   She had written to her seven children and told them. "I said that I was leaving their father. I did not tell them where I was going." She looked through the letters from the mailbox. There were no letters from her children that day, but there was a check from a lawyer in Illinois. It was a check for $10,000.

95 It was from an uncle she had taken care of through a long illness. She took the check as a sign. She was supposed to leave Joe. She used the money to start her life over.

Katy didn't know where she was going. She simply knew that she had to leave. For a month she lived in her car. She

100 moved from place to place so Joe couldn't find her. Then she got a job taking care of a widowed doctor's house and cooking meals. For her work, she got a room and meals. In the evenings she took classes at the nearby college. Eventually she found a full-time job. She worked in all the positions in a social work

105 office, and soon she was the supervisor. She was 66 years old when she finished her master's degree in education. That was one year past her goal of finishing before 65.

Katy says that besides the births of her children, there have been some great moments in her life. For example, at

110 the age of 55, she got her first hearing aid. For the first time she heard the tick of a watch and the songs of birds. Her graduation was another great moment. And so were some of the moments in her work. She worked with families in trouble, just as hers had been. She helped people through

115 their difficulties. Katy helped her children get educations, and she supported them through many hard times. Now she has three great-grandchildren. Katy is a senior citizen, but she says, "In my heart, I'm still eighteen."

120   If you ask her about Joe, she is kind. "He needed to be sick and to live as a sick man. I needed to be happy." If you ask her about her children, she says, "I have always wanted to live until my children didn't need me anymore. But I have to keep on living, because they still need me."

Words and Idioms List

You already know some of these words and idioms. Go through the list. Write a check (✓) next to each of those that you do not know.

Some of these words and idioms may be completely new for you. Find them in the reading. Use the sentences around them to understand what they mean. Note how they are used. These are the words and idioms to learn for this story.

1. _____ to **argue** (verb): to have a fight with words; to disagree

2. _____ **asparagus** (non-count noun): a spear-like green vegetable

3. _____ **charming** (adjective): pleasant in personality

4. _____ **cranberries** (plural noun): sour berries that are used to make a sauce

5. _____ a **dairy cow** (noun): an animal that gives lots of milk

6. _____ to **deliver** (verb): to take to a person, or to help a woman give birth to (a child)

7. _____ **depressed** (adjective): very sad in spirit

8. _____ a **disagreement** (noun): a fight with words

9. _____ to **enlist** (verb): to join

10. _____ to **enroll** (verb): to become a student

11. _____ to **graduate** (verb): to finish studies at a school; to get a degree or diploma

12. _____ **gravy** (non-count noun): a sauce made with meat juices, seasonings, and flour

13. _____ **harsh** (adjective): difficult to tolerate; severe; hard

14. _____ a **hearing impairment** (noun): a lack of ability to hear sounds

15. _____ to **intend** (verb): to plan; to mean for something to be (that way)

16. _____ a **legal paper** (noun): a document that can be used in court

17. _____ a **navy** (noun): an armed force that deals with ships

18. _____ a **parish priest** (noun): a spiritual leader of a community or church

19. _____ a **patient** (noun): a person who is sick and in the hospital

20. _____ a **photograph album** (noun): a book into which pictures from a camera are put

21. _____ **psychologically** (adverb): in or of the mind

22. _____ a **quit claim** (noun): a legal paper in which a person gives up property

23. _____ a **realization** (noun): an understanding of the facts

24. _____ **rights** (plural noun): the ability to own something, the ability to vote, and the like

25. _____ a **senior citizen** (noun): a person over the age of 65

26. _____ a **supervisor** (noun): a boss; a person in charge

27. _____ **undaunted** (adjective): not stopped

28. _____ a **veteran** (noun): a retired soldier

29. _____ **wounded** (adjective): hurt in battle

30. _____ **wrinkled** (adjective): not smooth, but creased with many lines (said of old people's skin)

After You Have Read the Story

Do you have the answers to the questions from "While You Read the Story"? Talk about the answers with your classmates.

Understanding Sequence

In the blank in front of each sentence, write 2–12 to show that you know the order of the story.

a. _____ She went to Europe as an Army nurse.

b. _____ Katy decided that she had to leave.

c. __1__ Katy was born in Pocahontas, Illinois in 1923.

d. _____ She was transferred to the Southwest.

e. _____ Katy met a man named Joe, fell in love, and married him.

f. _____ The harsh conditions in wartime Europe made her sick.

g. _____ She went to one nursing school and then another.

h. _____ She graduated from nursing school in 1944.

i. _____ They had seven children in nine years.

j. _____ Joe became very depressed and started to drink a lot.

k. _____ She got a job and started going to a university.

l. _____ She graduated with a master's degree in education when she was 66.

Answering Questions About the Story

Read these questions, think about the answers, and then discuss the answers with your classmates.

1. When is it right for a husband and wife to separate?

2. What did Joe do that showed his feeling about his marriage?

3. Why do you think Katy took her photograph albums with her when she left?

4. What happened on Thanksgiving Day that helped Katy make her decision?

5. What does Katy remember about her mother?

6. Why did Betty and Katy want to join the Navy?

7. Why did Katy choose to work as a nurse at night?

8. What is a quit claim? Why did Joe want her to sign it?

9. What did Joe do with his quit claim?

10. Why did Katy live in her car for a month?

Drawing Conclusions from the Story

Which of these statements is probably true, from the information in the story? Find a sentence in the story that shows each sentence is true or false. Write *true* or *false* in the blank in front of each sentence.

1. _____ Katy didn't have much education.

2. _____ The Great Lakes Naval Base has a big hospital.

3. _____ Soldiers are wounded in wars.

4. _____ There are special hospitals for soldiers who have been hurt.

5. _____ It was harder to get into the Navy than the Army.

6. _____ Dry air is good for people who get some kinds of diseases.

7. _____ Katy listened to the advice of her children to leave Joe.

8. _____ Joe wasn't happy in his marriage.

9. _____ Popcorn can grow in Illinois.

10. _____ A hearing aid can help a person with a hearing impairment.

Finding the Meaning in Context

Which meaning is closest to the underlined word or words? Circle *a, b, c,* or *d.*

1. The two people never had <u>an argument</u>.

    a. a disagreement   c. an impairment

    b. rights   d. a realization

2. Katy had many difficulties in her life, but she was <u>not going to let difficulties stop her</u>.
   a. wrinkled   c. graduated
   b. depressed   d. undaunted

3. Katy went to a nursing school and <u>signed up for classes</u>.
   a. enlisted   c. argued
   b. enrolled   d. delivered

4. The weather in that part of the world was <u>cold and damp</u>.
   a. depressed   c. harsh
   b. wrinkled   d. tick

5. The nurses took care of the <u>sick and wounded people</u> in the hospital.
   a. patients   c. doctors
   b. nurses   d. veterans

6. The <u>understanding</u> that she had to leave came to her on Thanksgiving Day.
   a. imperfect   c. argument
   b. realization   d. disagreement

7. Betty <u>joined</u> the Navy.
   a. enlisted in   c. walked out of
   b. intended to   d. fought in

8. She was 55 years old before she heard the <u>sound</u> of a watch.
   a. carrot   c. tick
   b. quit   d. song

Matching New Words and Meanings

Draw a line between the two words or phrases with similar meanings.

1. sad		a.	husband
2. suitcase		b.	nurse
3. join		c.	graduate
4. disagree		d.	bag
5. letter		e.	enlist
6. woman		f.	legal paper
7. doctor		g.	mail
8. check		h.	veteran
9. listen		i.	depressed
10. document		j.	children
11. soldier		k.	argue
12. man		l.	money
13. sons and daughters		m.	wife
14. finish school		n.	hear

Practicing with Idioms

Find the word or phrase in this list that means the same or almost the same as the underlined idiom and write it in the blank.

hearing impairment	wounded
psychologically	veterans
quit claims	gravy
was talented	enlist

1. Betty and Katy wanted to <u>join the Navy</u>.

   Betty and Katy wanted to _____ .

2. Joe brought home two <u>legal documents</u> to sign.

   Joe brought home two _____ to sign.

3. Her husband was a charming person who <u>could do many different things well</u>.

   Her husband was a charming person who _____ .

4. A lot of people were <u>hurt badly</u> during the war.

   A lot of people were _____ during the war.

5. <u>In her mind</u>, she was strong.

   _____ , she was strong.

6. He went to a hospital for <u>soldiers who served in armed forces</u>.

   He went to a hospital for _____ .

7. The man had a <u>problem with hearing</u>.

   The man had a _____ .

8. They asked for mashed potatoes with <u>a sauce made from meat juices</u>.

   They asked for mashed potatoes with _____ .

Expanding Vocabulary

In this list, there are really two separate lists. Some are personal items, and the others are the names of foods. Write the words and phrases in two separate lists.

milk	letters	melons	watches
shoes	purses	wallets	cranberries
beans	carrots	brushes	make-up
gravy	lettuce	suitcases	legal papers
combs	pencils	asparagus	photograph albums
popcorn	clothing	hearing aid	

Personal Items	Foods

Add some other personal items and the names of more foods to the two lists.

Exploring the Ideas

Think about these questions. Talk about your opinions with your classmates.

1. A person who cannot hear has a serious problem. It is not easy to learn how to speak if one cannot hear. What help can a hearing-impaired person get?

2. The Army and the Navy are similar. How are they alike? How are they different?

3. Why are there special hospitals for soldiers and veterans?

4. What is your opinion about arguments? Are they always bad? When are they good?

5. Why are some people homeless? Who helps the homeless?

Making Inferences

A. Answer these questions.

1. How do we know that Joe didn't give the lawyer the paper that he signed?

2. Why was Katy "an imperfect child" in her parents' opinion?

3. Why did Katy ask their family doctor for help in finding a nursing school?

4. Why couldn't Katy and Joe ever work out their problems?

5. What sign did Katy get that it was right to leave Joe?

6. Why did Katy want to finish her master's degree one year before she did?

7. Why is Katy a senior citizen?

B. Read the numbered sentence. Then read the sentences under it. Which ones are true because the numbered sentence is true? Circle the letter in front of each true statement.

1. Katy worked in a social work office.

   a. Katy wanted to help families in trouble.

   b. Katy couldn't find any other job.

   c. Katy had the necessary education for the job.

   d. Katy liked working with doctors and lawyers.

2. There have been some great moments in Katy's life.

    a. She was born in Illinois.

    b. She went to nursing school.

    c. She went to Europe as an Army nurse.

    d. She found a lot of money in the mail.

    e. She had seven children.

3. Katy is a senior citizen.

    a. She is over 65 years of age.

    b. She has seven children.

    c. She has a master's degree.

    d. She lives in Illinois.

    e. She lives in Europe.

4. Her family grew their own food.

    a. They were self-sufficient.

    b. They had a garden with lots of vegetables.

    c. They had good educations.

    d. They all worked hard.

5. Joe was a talented but unhappy man.

    a. He was charming to everyone but his family.

    b. He began to drink a lot.

    c. He laughed a lot.

    d. Joe was a wounded soldier who could not be happy.

Finding the Main Ideas

Here is a list of nine ideas. They are supporting ideas for the main ideas in the boxes at the top of the columns. Write each one in the box under the main idea that it supports.

1. Joe was a talented man who was very unhappy.
2. Katy graduated from nursing school, enlisted as an Army nurse, and went to Europe.

3. Katy had trouble becoming a nurse because of her hearing.

4. She could see that Joe was drinking too much.

5. A farm girl in the 1940s could go to nursing school or a teachers' college.

6. Katy left home with three suitcases and her photograph albums.

7. She realized that she could not be happy living with Joe.

8. Katy went back to school.

9. Katy found a job taking care of a house.

Main idea 1:	**Main idea 2:**	**Main idea 3:**
Katy wanted to become a nurse and to see the world, but it wasn't easy for her.	Katy realized that she had to leave Joe and make a new life for herself.	Katy started her life over after her children were grown up.

Reading for Details

Find the answers to these questions in the story.

1. Katy was born in _____ , Illinois.

2. Katy's nurse friend was named _____ .

3. Katy's family earned _____ a day for the milk from their dairy cows.

4. Katy worked at a hospital in Europe for _____ months.

5. She was transferred to the _____ where the air is dry.

6. Katy left her husband in _____ .

7. Katy finished nursing school when she was _____ years old.

8. At the age of _____ , Katy got her first hearing aid.

9. Katy and Joe had _____ children.

10. Katy was _____ when she got her master's degree in education.

Taking a Close Look at the Meanings of the Words

1. A *quit claim* is a legal paper. Joe used it in a wrong way. He used it to steal from Katy. A person must always be careful to read a legal paper very carefully. Some of the letters are very small. That is called "the fine print." The fine print is often where the danger in legal papers can be found. Lawyers warn their clients: "Be sure to read the fine print."

2. Army nurses in wartime have very hard work. *Wounded* soldiers are hurt in battle. They get well because of the nurses' work. *Veterans' hospitals* take care of sick and wounded soldiers.

Living with Nature

Mother Nature provides for her children.
There is a way of life that is close to nature.

Before You Read the Story

Use these questions as preparation for reading the story. If you need to know the meaning of a word or idiom, check the Words and Idioms List after the story.

1. What things did the McCarthy family gather from nature?
2. What foods do we pay for that we could get for free from nature?
3. How is city life different from life outside a city?
4. Everything comes from nature—sometimes directly and sometimes not. What can a person collect or gather in nature to help that person live in comfort and in health?
5. How does a child learn about nature?
6. What are the four seasons, and why are they important to a person living in nature?

While You Read the Story

Read these questions and look for the answers as you read the story.

1. How is Ella learning about nature?
2. How did her parents become in touch with nature?
3. What does the family have to buy?
4. This story takes place more than fifty years ago. How do you know? Look for ways that life was different then. Could this story happen today? Why or why not? If so, where?

Living with Nature

1   Growing up in the middle of a huge forest in Ontario
meant Ella McCarthy was in touch with nature. She learned
the names of the wildflowers in the woods and meadows.
She learned the names of the trees. In the early spring, Ella
5   picked little dandelion leaves for salad. From the stream, her
mother brought home watercress. These greens were made
into delicious salads. By the end of May, Ella and her father
looked for berries on the Juneberry tree. They picked the
plump berries and took them home for a fine sauce. Next the
10   pin cherries were ripe for picking. They picked these tiny
bright red fruits from a tree in a meadow near the town. No
one else wanted the pin cherries, except some birds, so Ella
and her father picked them for cherry juice. These cherries
were sour but full of vitamins, her father said. The McCarthys
15   drank the juice to prevent colds.

In the summer, Ella went with her father to
pick wild strawberries, raspberries, blueberries,
and blackberries. They took the berries home
in baskets, sat at the kitchen table, and
20   cleaned them. Bits of leaves and stems
went into a pile, and the cleaned berries
went into an iron pot with sugar. Ella's
mother cooked the berries and made

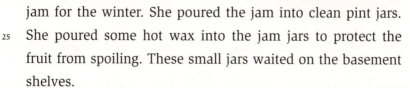

jam for the winter. She poured the jam into clean pint jars.
25   She poured some hot wax into the jam jars to protect the
fruit from spoiling. These small jars waited on the basement
shelves.

In the fall, Ella and her father went to the wild apple
trees in the woods. They collected the fruit and carried home

30 bushel baskets full of apples. They peeled the apples for canning. Ella's mother prepared the glass jars, and when the apples were cooked, apples for winter pies and applesauce went into the jars. The gleaming quart jars of apples went to the shelves in the basement too, for winter meals. They
35 preserved the fruit for later use.

A month later, the wild nuts were ready to be gathered. The McCarthys knew where there were hazelnut bushes, and

every year they picked the bushes clean before the squirrels took them all. They also picked
40 the rose hips from the wild rosebushes. These rose hips made a very good winter tea, and they had lots of vitamins in them. Ella loved the taste of the rose hip tea. It was a dark red color, and it tasted wonderful with honey.

45 Fall was also the time for collecting wood for the winter. The McCarthys gathered dead wood, of course, and had a pile of logs ready to burn. They also gathered pine knots. Several years earlier, there had been a forest fire near the Pine River. Ella's family planned picnics there every fall.
50 They went to pick up the pine knots. The area where the fire had burned was several acres in size, and all the pine trees there had burned. But the places on the tree where the big branches grew out from the trunk were harder than the rest of the wood. These parts had not burned. These small pieces
55 of wood lay on the grass and in the sand, sometimes partly buried. Ella, her mother, her father, and her younger brothers all collected the pine knots in bags. They piled the pine knots into the little trailer that was hitched to the back of the car. Those pine knots would burn slowly all winter in the furnace
60 and keep them all warm.

One fall, Ella's dad found a wild beehive in a dead tree. He covered himself with thick clothes. He put on a big hat with a strong net and heavy gloves. He put a smoking piece of wood into the middle of the tree, and most of the bees flew away. He collected two gallons of wild honey, but he left a lot of honey for the bees. He didn't like to rob the bees, but the wild honey tasted sweet. He got some bee  stings too, but the honey was worth it! Anyway, he said to himself, the bees had more honey than they needed.

In the winter, Ella was sometimes able to go fishing with her father. Of course, she had to go to school, but on weekends, they went to Ice Lake. The ice on this lake was four feet thick. It was cold for months at a time in their part of Canada. And there must have been millions of fish in that lake. Ella's father made a hole in the ice, and they lowered lines into the water.

The fish must have been hungry! They took the bait that Ella and her father put on their fishhooks. Their metal tubs were quickly filled with fish. Each person could take 100 fish home. Ella's father covered the fish in the tubs with snow. He tied ropes around the tubs, and together they pulled the tubs of fish to their car and took them home.

Then they had the job of cleaning the fish. Ella's father taught her how to remove the scales from the fish. Ella got very good at that part. But it can take a long time for one person to clean 100 fish, and twice as long to clean 200. So Ella's father taught her how to hold the fish, how to slit it up the belly with the tip of the knife, and how to scrape the fish clean. Soon Ella could keep up with her father, fish for fish.

When the fish were cleaned, they had to be washed and then wrapped in two kinds of paper. First Ella and her father laid about ten fish on a piece of waxed paper. The family usually ate ten fish for a meal, and they were making meal-size packages. Next that package went onto a piece of newspaper and was folded. The packages of fish were laid into a cardboard box in a neat way. The paper had to be dry. Otherwise all the packages would stick together. Then the box, covered with more newspaper, went into a gunnysack. Ella's dad put it on the roof to freeze. When the family wanted fish to eat, the packages of cleaned fish were ready.

Ella's family lived close to nature. They depended on nature for much of their food. They needed the forest to be able to live in comfort. They didn't think that their way of life was unusual. To them, it was how all people should live.

Words and Idioms List

You already know some of these words and idioms. Go through the list. Write a check (✓) next to each of those that you do not know.

Some of these words and idioms may be completely new for you. Find them in the reading. Use the sentences around them to understand what they mean. Note how they are used. These are the words and idioms to learn for this story.

1. _____ **bait** (non-count noun): food used to catch animals such as fish or mice

2. _____ a **beehive** (noun): a home for a community of bees, where there is a lot of honey

3. _____ to **be in touch with** (idiom): to communicate with easily; to be familiar with

4. _____ a **belly** (noun): the lower abdomen of an animal; the underside of a fish

5. _____ to **be worth it** (idiom): to give a good value in exchange for it

6. _____ a **bushel basket** (noun): a container made of wood strips that can hold a bushel measure (32 quarts, or 35.24 dry liters)

7. _____ to **collect** (verb): to gather; to pick up and bring to one place

8. _____ a **dandelion** (noun): a weed with bright yellow flowers, the leaves of which can be eaten as salad

9. _____ to **fish** (verb): to catch fish for food

10. _____ a **fishhook** (noun): a curved wire with a sharp barb on the end for catching fish to eat

11. _____ to **freeze** (verb): to become solid from cold

12. _____ a **furnace** (noun): a central place for heating a building

13. _____ to **gather** (verb): to pick up and bring to one place; to collect

14. _____ **gleaming** (adjective): shiny

15. _____ a **glove** (noun): a cloth or leather covering for a hand

16. _____ **greens** (plural noun): leaves for salad

17. _____ to **hitch** (verb): to attach or connect so as to be able to pull

18. _____ a **jar** (noun): a glass container with a large opening at the top, or mouth

19. _____ a **log** (noun): a large piece of wood cut from a tree

20. _____ a **metal tub** (noun): a large container made of coated iron, used for washing clothes or holding water

21. _____ **nature** (non-count noun): all the world, especially what people have not changed

22. _____ to **peel** (verb): to remove the skin of (fruit or vegetables) with a knife

23. _____ a **pine knot** (noun): a hard piece of unburned wood from a burned tree from the place where a branch and tree trunk separated

24. _____ **plump** (adjective): fat and juicy

25. _____ **ripe** (adjective): ready to be used or eaten

26. _____ to **rob** (verb): to take from; to steal from

27. _____ a **rose hip** (noun): the hard, round fruit of a rose plant

28. _____ **scales** (plural noun): the thin, clear, round, pearl-like disks that cover the body of a cold-water fish (Scales need to be removed before the fish can be eaten.)

29. _____ to **scrape** (verb): to use a hard tool to remove something on the surface of another thing

30. _____ to **slit** (verb): to cut with a knife in a straight line

31. _____ a **stem** (noun): the green part between a fruit and the roots

32. _____ a **sting** (noun): a painful bite or sore from a bee or other insect

33. _____ a **trailer** (noun): a wheeled cart that can be pulled by a car or truck

34. _____ **watercress** (non-count noun): a salad green plant of tasty leaves that grows at the edge of streams

35. _____ **wax** (non-count noun): paraffin; candle wax

After You Have Read the Story

Do you have the answers to the questions from "While You Read the Story"? Talk about the answers with your classmates.

Understanding Sequence

In the blank in front of each sentence, write 2–6 to show that you know the order of the job of making jam and 2–7 to show that you understand the job of ice fishing.

The Job of Making Jam

a. _____ Cook the berries with sugar.

b. _____ Find berries in the woods.

c. _____ Pour the jam into jars.

d. _____ Pick the berries

e. __1__ Go to the open areas of the woods where berries grow.

f. _____ Clean the leaves and stems from the berries.

The Job of Ice Fishing

a. _____ Cut a hole in the lake ice.

b. _____ Wait for a fish to take the bait.

c. __1__ Go to a lake.

d. _____ Put bait on the fishhook.

e. _____ Pull up the line and the fish.

f. _____ Lower the line with the hook into the water.

g. _____ Put the fish into the tub.

Answering Questions About the Story

Read these questions, think about the answers, and then discuss the answers with your classmates.

1. Where did Ella live?
2. Who ate the pin cherries? (Give two answers.)
3. What did the squirrels collect?
4. Where do hazelnuts grow?
5. What are the names of the seasons?
6. What did Ella and her family do in each season?
7. Where did they get apples?
8. Where does honey come from?
9. Where was the forest fire? What did it leave behind?
10. How did Ella and her father preserve the fish?

Drawing Conclusions from the Story

Which of these statements are probably true, from the information in the story? Write *true* or *false* in the blank in front of each sentence.

1. _____ Ella lived in an apartment in a city.
2. _____ Pin cherry juice is very sweet.
3. _____ Jam tastes sweet.
4. _____ Squirrels like nuts.
5. _____ Rose hip tea is sour.
6. _____ Bees live in a beehive.
7. _____ The wood in pine knots is heavier than the wood in a pine tree log.
8. _____ The winter in Ontario is quite cold.
9. _____ Ella's family could eat twenty fish in one meal.
10. _____ It was very cold on the roof of the house in the winter.

Finding the Meaning in Context

Which meaning is closest to the underlined word or words? Circle *a, b, c,* or *d*.

1. The family owned a trailer to <u>attach</u> to the back of the car.
   a. collect   c. scrape
   b. hitch   d. slit

2. Ella's mother went to a stream to collect <u>a salad green</u>.
   a. watercress   c. berries
   b. dandelions   d. gloves

3. Ella's father didn't like <u>taking honey from</u> the bees.
   a. smoking   c. burning
   b. finding   d. robbing

4. Ella <u>was in touch with</u> nature.
   a. lived in   c. was busy because of
   b. didn't like   d. was comfortable with

5. When the weather is extremely cold, water <u>turns solid</u>.
   a. scrapes   c. freezes
   b. stops   d. piles

6. The best berries are round and <u>full of juice</u>.
   a. wild   c. plump
   b. sour   d. thick

7. To preserve apples, you must <u>remove their skins</u>.
   a. peel them   c. scrape them
   b. cook them   d. clean them

8. The jars must be <u>shining clean</u>.
   a. prepared   c. burned
   b. gleaming   d. cooked

9. The apples were <u>ready for picking</u>.
   a. sweet   c. plump
   b. sour   d. ripe

10. They made tea with <u>the fruit of wild rosebushes</u>.
    a. leaves
    c. stems
    b. rose hips
    d. vitamins

Working with New Words and Meanings

Which word or phrase from this list answers the question? In the blank in front of each question, write the letter of the answer.

a. a log	g. a stem
b. a jar	h. a sting
c. jam	i. scraping
d. bait	j. dandelion
e. belly	k. watercress
f. gloves	l. a bushel basket

1. _____ What can protect your hands from the cold?

2. _____ What do you put on a fishhook to attract the fish?

3. _____ What is a measure for potatoes?

4. _____ What is a bite from a bee or a mosquito?

5. _____ What is like a bottle but has a large opening at the top?

6. _____ What do you get when you cook berries with sugar?

7. _____ What word means the stomach of an animal or the underside of a fish?

8. _____ Which is the name of a salad green that grows near streams?

9. _____ What do we call a piece of wood cut from a tree?

10. _____ The leaves of which weed with yellow flowers can be used for salad?

11. _____ What connects the apple to the tree?

12. _____ If you use the sharp edge of a knife to take scales from a fish, what are you doing?

Practicing with Idioms

Find the idiom in this list that means the same or almost the same as the underlined word or words and use the correct form of it to complete each sentence.

to be in touch with   to be ripe for picking
to live close to   to plan a picnic
to be worth it   way of life
to be the time for   to be very good at

1. On Sunday afternoons, the family often <u>arranged to eat a meal</u> in the forest.

   On Sunday afternoons, the family often _____ in the forest.

2. In September, the apples on the trees are <u>ready to be collected</u>.

   In September, the apples on the trees are _____ .

3. The children of the family are <u>familiar with many of the aspects of</u> nature.

   The children of the family are _____ nature.

4. The family went fifty miles to fish on Ice Lake, and they caught 400 fish. It was a lot of work, but <u>the reward for the work was valuable for them</u>.

   The family went fifty miles to fish on Ice Lake, and they caught 400 fish. It was a lot of work, but _____ .

5. Collecting what they need from nature is <u>how they live</u>.

   Collecting what they need from nature is their _____ .

6. Mr. McCarthy is <u>skilled in</u> fishing.

   Mr. McCarthy _____ fishing.

7. Some people <u>depend on</u> nature <u>for food and fuel</u>.

   Some people _____ nature.

8. Spring <u>is the appropriate season</u> for planting flowers in a garden.

   Spring _____ for planting flowers in a garden.

Exploring the Ideas

Think about these questions. Talk about your opinions with your classmates.

1. The McCarthy family had to be in touch with nature. They needed to know how to survive, to live in the forest. Mr. McCarthy cut wood to sell. He also had a job with the government, in the forest. However, the family did not earn much money. What did they do to survive?

2. How many people do you think are in the McCarthy family's community? Why do you think as you do? What kind of work might they have?

3. How do the McCarthys heat their home in cold weather? Could everyone do the same?

4. How did the family save food for the winter? What do people do today to preserve food?

5. What is Ella learning from her parents about living with nature?

6. Fish is mostly winter food for the McCarthy family. Why?

7. Which fruits have a lot of vitamins?

8. Bees make honey from the pollen of flowers. The honey is really food for baby bees. Bees also make wax. The wax holds the honey in small pockets within the beehive. What uses do people have for honey and wax?

Making Inferences

Read the numbered sentence. Then read the sentences under it. Which ones are true because the numbered sentence is true? Circle the letter in front of each true statement.

1. Pin cherry juice is sour, but it has a lot of vitamins in it.
    a. The McCarthys drank pin cherry juice to prevent colds.
    b. The McCarthys added sugar or honey to pin cherry juice.
    c. Sour fruits contain vitamins.
    d. The children didn't drink the juice.
    e. Sometimes people drink things because they are good for them.

2. They took the berries home and cleaned them.
    a. They couldn't clean the berries in the woods.
    b. The berries were dirty.
    c. There were leaves and stems in the basket with the berries.
    d. Berries have to be clean to make them into jam.

3. Each person who went fishing on Ice Lake could take home 100 fish.
    a. There were a lot of fishermen on the lake.
    b. The lake had millions of fish in it.
    c. Not many people went ice fishing.
    d. The people who went ice fishing needed fish for food.
    e. Ice Lake was not a popular place to fish.
    f. There are rules about the number of fish that a person can catch in one day.
    g. It was good for a family that needed food to go fishing as a group.

4. The family could eat ten fish for a meal, and they were making meal-size packages.
    a. Each person could eat three fish at one meal.
    b. The fish were very, very large.
    c. There were ten people in the family.
    d. They wrapped ten fish at a time.
    e. Each package held enough for one meal.
    f. The McCarthys eat only fish.

5. The places on a pine tree where the big branches grow out from the trunk are "knots," and the wood of a pine knot is harder than the rest of the wood.

   a. Pine knots are just like any wood from a pine tree.

   b. Pine knots come from branches of pine trees.

   c. It takes more heat to start a pine knot burning than any other part of the tree.

   d. A pine knot is like a twisted place on a rope.

Finding the Main Ideas

Choose the best answer.

1. Which of these sentences from paragraph 1 shows that Ella was in touch with nature?

   a. They picked the plump berries and took them home for a fine sauce.

   b. The family drank the juice to prevent colds.

   c. No one wanted the pin cherries, except some birds.

   d. She learned the names of the wildflowers in the woods and meadows.

2. Which of these sentences is the main idea for the things they did in the fall?

   a. The fall was a time to pick wildflowers and berries.

   b. The fall was the time to collect fruits, nuts, and wood.

   c. The fall was a time to rest and go on picnics.

   d. The fall was the time to gather berries for jam.

3. Which of these sentences explains why pine knots are valuable?

   a. Pine knots lie on the grass or half buried in the sand.

   b. Pine knots will never burn.

   c. Pine knots come from the places where branches grow out of a tree trunk.

   d. Pine knots are hard, so they will burn hot in a furnace.

4. Which of these sentences explains why ice fishing is easy?

   a. A person can take home 100 fish.

   b. There are many fish under the ice and not much food, so they go for the bait.

   c. The ice on the lake is four feet deep.

   d. The fish are quite small, so it takes 100 fish to feed a person.

5. Which of these titles is appropriate for this story?

   a. Learning About Nature in a Classroom

   b. How a Family Survived with the Help of Nature

   c. Finding the Honey in the Hole in the Tree

   d. Wild Life

Reading for Details

Find the answers to these questions in the story.

1. What color is rose hip tea?

2. When do Juneberries become ripe?

3. Why did the family go to the Pine River for their picnic?

4. What did the McCarthys use apples for?

Taking a Close Look at the Meanings of the Words

1. The word *canning* is used for preserving fruits and vegetables. Of course, the foods that we buy in stores are *in cans*. However, the noun *canning* and the verb *to can* are also used for preserving food in jars. It is necessary to *sterilize* everything that will be canned. *Sterilizing* means killing all the germs, so jars are put into boiling water. The heat of the water cleans the jars. The filled jars are *sealed* so that no air can get inside. Then the food inside these *sterile* jars will not spoil.

2. There are many words in this story for containers: *jar, bottle, basket, bag, cardboard box, bucket, pail, tub*. What other words do you know for containers? What is stored in each container?

3. Fruit can be made into jam, sauce, or juice. Jam is thick and sugary. Juice can be drunk. And sauce is usually eaten with another food.

4. The verbs *to lie* and *to lay* are often confused by native speakers and English learners alike. Here are some sentences with these two verbs.

   To lie (lie, lay, lain)

   - After working all day, it is nice to *lie* down and rest.
   - Last night I *lay* down at about ten o'clock.
   - I must have *lain* there for an hour before I fell asleep.

   To lay (lay, laid, laid)

   - I always *lay* my books on the table near the door when I come from school.
   - I know that I *laid* my books there last night.
   - I found my books in the kitchen, so I must have *laid* them down there.

   The difficulty comes because the past tense of *to lie* is the same in appearance as the present tense of *to lay*. The difference in meaning is that *to lay (something)* means "to put or place (something)." *To lie* means "to recline oneself."

Magic?

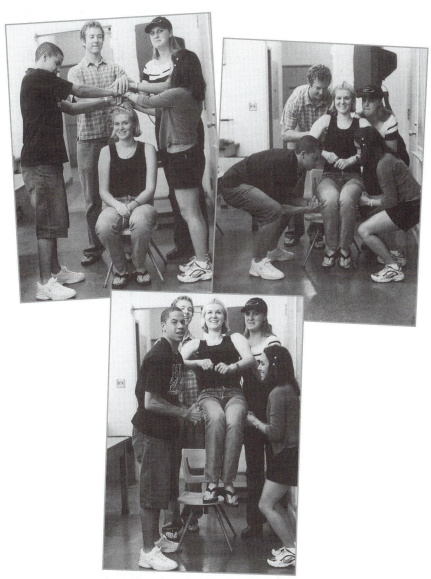

Kelly sits on a chair. First four classmates put their hands on her head. Then they lift her, using only their eight index fingers. Is it magic?

Before You Read the Story

Use these questions as preparation for reading the story. If you need to know the meaning of a word or idiom, check the Words and Idioms List after the story.

1. The name of this story is "Magic?" Look at the pictures and then look at this list of words. Which ones do you expect to be in this unit? Why? Circle them.

spoon	doctor	brain	trick	pain
eyes	bag	blood	sore	heal
headache	fork	salt	believe	fingers
elbow	surprise	ankle	oxygen	burn
knee				

2. Do you think the storyteller believes in magic? Why or why not?

3. Who "does" magic?

4. What is most magic?

While You Read the Story

Read these questions and look for the answers as you read the story.

1. What unusual and unexpected things did the storyteller see?

2. Why isn't the hegu point magical to the storyteller?

3. Why is the lifting of a person on eight fingers somewhat magical?

4. What could the title "Mind Over Metal" be used for?

Magic?

1   There are some things in the universe that are beyond our understanding. One of those things is how I bent spoons with the energy of my mind. I was at a workshop about not limiting ourselves by our doubts. Each

5   participant had a regular spoon. We were to hold our spoons lightly and then think about making them bend. We were to think about the metal getting soft. The leader told us that

10   when the spoon started to bend, we

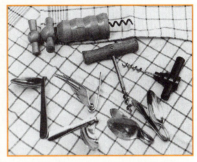

were to say, "It's bending!" Until then we were to say, "Bend! Bend! Bend!" I doubted that a spoon would listen to me.

Then as I was holding the spoon and putting hardly any pressure on it, the spoon began to turn in my hand. To my

15   surprise, the spoon got soft and bent into a 90-degree angle. I started to say, "It's bending!" And others looked at me, still saying, "Bend! Bend!" I looked around. Suddenly other people's spoons were bending into loops. I picked up another spoon, as the leader asked me, "Why don't you believe?"

20   And this time, the spoon did what I instructed it to do. It bent over double into a full loop and then some. The third time, I picked up a fork instead of a spoon. I believed that the metal would get soft, and when it began to bend, I turned it in all ways. I twisted it twice and made a corkscrew

25   out of it. It was thrilling to see that a law of nature could be broken, or at least bent.

I saw another really strange thing happen. Four people picked up a fifth person without any strain. The procedure is simple: one person sits on a chair. The four people can try to

30 pick up the person in the chair by holding onto one chair leg
each and lifting. That way, however, is not easy. The better
way is to defy gravity. The four lifters put their hands, one
on top of the other, on top of the head of the person on the
chair. Then they press down gently with all eight hands.
35 Then, on the count of three, they remove their hands, and
with their index fingers only, lift the person. Two put their
fingers under the person's knees. The other two put their
index fingers under the person's shoulders, in the armpits.
And all lift together. The eight fingers of the four lifters will
40 raise the person off the chair and into the air.

Is it magic? Or it is something else? There are some
things that are simply mysterious. We do not know why they
work. To many people, acupuncture and acupressure are in
the category of the unknown. One day, I was teaching a
45 graduate class in methodology, and a student in the front
row was pulsing with headache pain. He didn't say anything

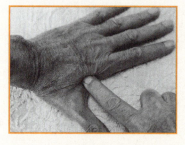

about it, but I could see the pain
coming from him. I continued to
teach, but I went to the student's
50 side. His eyes were closed. I put
out my hand. Without opening
his eyes, he put his hand in
mine. I touched a point on the back of his hand opposite his
thumb. I began to rub that point, the hegu point. Tears ran
55 down his face, but I continued the gentle massage of the
hegu point on his hand. And I continued to talk to the class
about teaching English as a second language. Suddenly, the
man opened his eyes and smiled. "It's gone!" he said. "My
headache is gone. What did you do?"

60 I assured him that there was no magic. There are two circulation systems in the body, I told him. One is the blood. Blood carries oxygen and nutrients or food to the cells of the body. The other circulation system is electrical. Calcium, magnesium, potassium, and salts, like table salt or sodium,
65 carry the electrical signals from the brain to parts of the body. The hegu point is the place where the lines or tensions of the electrical system for the head and the upper part of the body cross. A person who has a headache probably has
70 congestion there. The congestion causes the hegu point to be very, very sore. However, if the point is rubbed until it is not sore anymore, the headache will go away.

"I thought you were some kind of heavenly doctor," the student said after class. "I don't remember ever having such
75 a bad headache before. But what other points of the body are as powerful in healing as the hegu point?"

I said that I was no Chinese doctor, but I knew a few things. I had accidentally found a spot on the outside of my arm that helped my bowels. I knew that there was a special
80 spot on my arm, two inches from the point halfway between the pit of my elbow and the tip of the joint bone. This point on my right arm helped my left knee. On the left arm, it helped the right knee. Another spot, on my ankle, helped back and leg pain. There is no magic in acupressure, so the
85 bending of spoons and the lifting with fingers must have explanations too. We simply don't know what they are yet.

Words and Idioms List

You already know some of these words and idioms. Go through the list. Write a check (✓) next to each of those that you do not know.

Some of these words and idioms may be completely new for you. Find them in the reading. Use the sentences around them to understand what they mean. Note how they are used. These are the words and idioms to learn for this story.

1. _____ **acupressure** (non-count noun): the science of healing by pressing special spots on the body; part of Chinese medicine

2. _____ **acupuncture** (non-count noun): the science of healing by inserting very thin needles into special spots of the body; part of Chinese medicine

3. _____ an **armpit** (noun): the part of the body under the shoulder joint

4. _____ to **assure someone** (verb): to promise or swear to someone that something is true; to guarantee; to make someone feel secure in the news about something

5. _____ to **bend** (verb): to cause to turn at an angle

6. _____ **bowels** (plural noun): the digestive system (the stomach, the intestines, and so on)

7. _____ **congestion** (non-count noun): a place where fluids gather; thickness

8. _____ a **corkscrew** (noun): a tool used to remove a cork from a bottle

9. _____ to **defy** (verb): to disobey; to challenge

10. _____ a **doubt** (noun): a feeling of not believing; disbelief

11. _____ to **doubt** (verb): to not believe; to disbelieve

12. _____ **energy** (non-count noun): force; strength

13. _____ **gravity** (non-count noun): the force of nature that gives things weight

14. _____ an **index finger** (noun): the finger next to the thumb; the pointing finger

15. _____ a **law of nature** (noun): an explanation of how things work in the world; a principle

16. _____ a **loop** (noun): a circle or oval shape

17. _____ a **massage** (noun): a rubdown by a person skilled in rubbing the muscles to bring about relaxation

18. _____ to **massage** (verb): to rub the muscles to bring about relaxation

19. _____ **mysterious** (adjective): not easily explained; not understood

20. _____ a **nutrient** (noun): an important element of food

21. _____ **pressure** (non-count noun): strength of pushing; force

22. _____ a **procedure** (noun): a process; a schedule of events that lead to a desired end

23. _____ **pulsing** (adjective): beating, like a heart or a drum

24. _____ **regular** (adjective): normal; not unusual

25. _____ **salts** (noun): the body's electrolytes: magnesium (Mg), sodium (Na), potassium (K), and calcium (Ca)

26. _____ **strain** (non-count noun): effort and tiredness of work

27. _____ to **twist** (verb): to turn in two directions

28. _____ **universe** (noun): the world and all the stars and planets

29. _____ a **workshop** (noun): a training session; a class for participants, not students

After You Have Read the Story

Do you have the answers to the questions from "While You Read the Story"? Talk about the answers with your classmates.

Understanding Sequence

A. There are three short stories within this one story. The first one is about bending spoons. In the blank in front of each sentence, write 2–6 to show that you know the order of the story about bending spoons.

   a. __1__   I went to a workshop called "Mind Over Metal."

   b. _____   I said, "Bend! Bend! Bend!" as I was told to do.

   c. _____   We were told to hold a spoon lightly and think about it bending.

   d. _____   Suddenly the spoon felt soft, and it bent into a loop.

   e. _____   I doubted that a spoon would listen to me.

   f. _____   I broke a law of nature with my mind.

B. In the blank in front of each sentence, write 2–9 to show that you know the order of the story about the lifting with fingers.

   a. _____   The four lifters put their hands on the head of the person in the chair and press down lightly.

   b. _____   Four people are chosen to be lifters.

   c. __1__   Five people volunteer to do the experiment.

   d. _____   That person sits in a chair.

   e. _____   One person is chosen to be lifted.

   f. _____   They quickly remove their hands from the person's head.

   g. _____   Two of them put their pointed index fingers under the person's knees.

   h. _____   They lift the person.

   i. _____   The other two put their index fingers under the person's shoulders.

C. In the blank in front of each sentence, write 2–6 to show that you know the order of the story about healing a headache with acupressure.

  a. _____ The headache goes away.

  b. __1__ First you must know that a person has a headache.

  c. _____ You press on the hegu point.

  d. _____ You pick up the person's hand.

  e. _____ You massage the hegu point until it stops hurting.

  f. _____ You find the hegu point on the side of the palm.

Answering Questions About the Story

Read these questions, think about the answers, and then discuss the answers with your classmates.

1. What was the storyteller doing at the spoon-bending workshop?
2. What happened to the fork?
3. What word did the spoon-benders have to say? Do you think the word has energy?
4. Why do you think the metal becomes soft?
5. Can you explain how eight fingers can lift a person who weighs 180 pounds?
6. What does a corkscrew look like?
7. What do the lifters have to do with their hands before they try to lift a person with their index fingers?
8. What force keeps a person sitting on a chair or standing on the ground?
9. What things are twisted?
10. Table salt is sodium chloride (NaCl). What things taste salty? Are they all sodium chloride?

Drawing Conclusions from the Story

Read the numbered sentence. Then read the sentences under it. Which ones are true because the numbered sentence is true? Circle the letter in front of each true statement.

1. There is no magic in acupressure, so the bending of spoons and the lifting with fingers must have explanations too.

    a. There is no explanation for acupressure.

    b. There is no explanation for the bending of spoons.

    c. There is no explanation for the lifting of a person with four people's index fingers.

    d. There must be explanations for all these things.

2. I believed that the metal would get soft, and when the fork began to bend, I turned it in all ways.

    a. The metal got soft enough to bend.

    b. I bent the fork.

    c. I twisted the fork.

3. I was at a workshop about not limiting ourselves by our doubts.

    a. People can learn to deal with their doubts.

    b. A workshop is a place to learn new things.

    c. We all have doubts.

    d. Doubts can stop a person from doing all the things that he or she could possibly do.

4. I doubted that a spoon would listen to me.

    a. Spoons have ears and can hear.

    b. I didn't believe the spoon would bend.

    c. I felt strong enough to bend a spoon.

    d. I did not believe the workshop leader.

5. Some things in nature are simply mysterious.

    a. We do not understand everything.

    b. We understand even mysterious things.

    c. Nature keeps secrets from us.

Finding the Meaning in Context

Which meaning is closest to the underlined word or words? Circle *a, b, c,* or *d.*

1. The thief put the valuable box <u>under his shoulder</u> to carry it away from the museum.

   a. on his elbow   c. in his hand

   b. in his ankle   d. in his armpit

2. I want to <u>promise</u> you that I will help you.

   a. assure   c. defy

   b. bend   d. press

3. A flu can make a person's <u>digestive system</u> hurt.

   a. bowels   c. pulsing

   b. congestion   d. regular

4. Vegetables provide valuable <u>elements of food</u> for the human body.

   a. salts   c. loops

   b. nutrients   d. oxygen

5. The <u>process</u> of baking a cake is quite simple.

   a. procedure   c. pulsing

   b. pressure   d. strain

6. I <u>do not believe</u> that this story in the newspaper is true.

   a. understand   c. doubt

   b. assure you   d. twist

7. When a person has a cold, there is <u>an accumulation of fluids</u> in his or her chest.

   a. a lot   c. a corkscrew

   b. a headache   d. congestion

8. The father shouted at his son, "How can you <u>go against</u> my wishes?"

   a. bend   c. defy

   b. assure   d. strain

9. If you <u>rub</u> a sore spot on your body, it will stop hurting and you will feel much better.

     a. pulse   c. strain

     b. massage   d. doubt

10. This book is nothing special; it is a <u>normal</u> dictionary.

     a. regular   c. unusual

     b. mysterious   d. fine

Matching New Words and Meanings

Draw a line between the two words or phrases with similar meanings.

1. massage		a. spot
2. knee		b. finger
3. bend		c. fork
4. circle		d. point
5. force		e. rub
6. ache		f. pain
7. tip		g. loop
8. place		h. elbow
9. thumb		i. twist
10. spoon		j. energy

Finding the Differences

What's the difference between …

1. a student in a class and a participant in a workshop?
2. a spoon and a fork?
3. a circle and a loop?
4. an index finger and a thumb?
5. understanding and doubt?
6. lift and raise?
7. to rub and to massage?

8. something being sore and something aching?

9. a knee and an elbow?

10. a point and a spot?

Practicing with Idioms

Find the idiom in this list that means the same or almost the same as the underlined word or words and use the correct form of it to complete each sentence. Note that some words (for example, [*one*]) can be replaced with other words and might be in another position in the sentence.

without any strain	and then some
be pulsing with	where lines cross
some kind of	there is no magic in
bend over double	be beyond [one's] understanding

1. <u>Nothing is mysterious about</u> the electrical system of the body.

   _____ the electrical system of the body.

2. It <u>is not something I can understand</u> that some people can choose to be unkind to others.

   It _____ that some people can choose to be unkind to others.

3. When the car was pulled out of the accident, it was <u>folded in half</u>.

   When the car was pulled out of the accident, it was

   _____ .

4. On main roads, there are traffic signs <u>where one road meets another</u>.

   On main roads, there are traffic signs _____ .

5. Everyone in the football stadium was shouting. The place <u>was filled with</u> excitement.

   Everyone in the football stadium was shouting. The place

   _____ excitement.

6. There was a lot of sickness in the town as <u>a variety of</u> flu.

   There was a lot of sickness in the town as _____ flu.

7. Tom has a lot of free time this week, so he can help at the school <u>and it won't be too much work for him</u>.

   Tom has a lot of free time this week, so he can help at the school

   _____ .

8. I spent twenty dollars <u>and more</u> for the ticket.

   I spent twenty dollars _____ for the ticket.

Exploring the Ideas

Think about these questions. Talk about your opinions with your classmates.

1. Gravity is one law of nature. What are some others? What are some of the effects of gravity? Think about fruit from a tree, water such as rain or water in a river, and the limits to a person's ability to run or climb. What law of nature was "bent" in the workshop?

2. What are spoons made of? Are they easy to bend? Why or why not?

3. What usually makes metal soft enough to twist?

4. Do you think that the experiment with acupressure defied a law of nature? If so, how? What?

5. What do you believe in, and what do you doubt? Think about your own abilities. Do you believe you could climb a mountain? Do you believe you could be an actor? What do you think is the truth about Chinese medicine? Have you ever had experiences that were unusual? Can you explain them?

Making Inferences

A. Read the numbered sentence. Then read the sentences under it. Which ones are true because the numbered sentence is true? Circle the letter in front of each true statement.

1. The storyteller says, "I am no Chinese doctor." What does the storyteller mean?

   a. The storyteller is Chinese.

   b. The storyteller is a doctor.

   c. The Chinese do not have doctors.

   d. Chinese doctors know about the hegu point.

   e. The storyteller knows some Chinese medicine, but not a lot.

2. Salts (such as calcium, sodium, magnesium, and potassium) carry electrical signals through the body.

   a. The human body has an electrical system.

   b. Potassium and magnesium have some things in common.

   c. There are calcium salts in a human body.

3. The hegu point is the crossing spot for the lines or tensions of the electrical system of the head and upper body.

   a. The hegu point is part of the lower body.

   b. A headache is related to the hegu point.

   c. There are lines along which electricity flows in the human body.

   d. The hegu point is in one's head.

4. We were to think about the metal getting soft.

   a. The storyteller needed to imagine the metal bending.

   b. The storyteller was strong enough to bend a spoon in his hand.

   c. The power of the mind could make the metal soft.

5. To many people, acupuncture and acupressure are in the category of the unknown.

   a. Everyone understands why acupuncture and acupressure work.

   b. There are some things that people do not understand.

   c. Acupressure is better than acupuncture.

   d. Acupuncture and acupressure seem to be magic.

B. Read the numbered sentence. Then read the sentences under it. Which sentence is closest in meaning to the numbered sentence? Circle *a, b, c,* or *d.*

1. It was thrilling to see that a law of nature could be broken, or at least bent.

   a. I was excited because I was doing something that should be impossible.

   b. I was enthusiastic about breaking spoons.

   c. I enjoyed playing with nature and making it do what I wanted.

2. The better way is to defy gravity.

   a. I prefer to be heavy in body and not be lifted.

   b. It is easier to do something to stop the normal pull of the earth on a body.

   c. I want to disobey all the laws of nature to do the job.

3. There are some things that are simply mysterious.

   a. There is nothing strange about magic.

   b. Simple things are not always easy to understand.

   c. We do not always understand everything.

4. I assured him that there was no magic in acupressure.

   a. Acupressure is a kind of magic.

   b. Acupressure is not magic.

   c. Magic is not part of my work.

Finding the Main Ideas and Supporting Ideas

One of the thirteen sentences below is the main idea for the whole article.

- Write *TH* (which means *thesis,* or main idea for an article or story) in the blank in front of that idea. Then write it on the appropriate line.

- There are three main topic ideas (one for each of the three topics). Write *MI* in the blank in front of each of those ideas. Then write each of them on the appropriate line.

- Finally, write the three sets of supporting ideas (SI) for each of the topics on the appropriate lines.

1. _____ It is possible to defy gravity.

2. _____ You hold the spoon lightly with just a little pressure on it.

3. _____ There are some things in the universe that we do not understand.

4. _____ Certain spots are congestion points for the electrical system of the body.

5. _____ You think about the spoon bending.

6. _____ Four people can lift a person from a chair using only their eight index fingers.

7. _____ Acupressure is a healing art, part of Chinese medicine.

8. _____ The spoon seems to become soft and bends into a loop.

9. _____ The lifters have to put their hands on the head of the person they will raise.

10. _____ The mind can bend a metal spoon.

11. _____ There is a point on one's hand where tension lines cross.

12. _____ They press down lightly before they try to lift.

13. _____ This point is called the hegu point.

Thesis: _____

_____

MI #1: _____

SI: _____

SI: _____

SI: _____

MI #2: _____

  SI: _____

  SI: _____

  SI: _____

MI #3: _____

  SI: _____

  SI: _____

  SI: _____

Reading for Details

Find the answers to these questions in the story.

1. When does a person say, "Bend! Bend! Bend!"?
2. How many fingers does it take to lift a person?
3. Where is the hegu point?
4. Which culture produced the arts of acupuncture and acupressure?
5. What are the two circulation systems of the human body?
6. What does the blood system do?
7. How do we know that there are other points like the hegu point?
8. Why is the hegu point sore when a person has a headache?
9. What can a person do about a headache without taking aspirin or some other pill?
10. Where are a person's armpits?

Taking a Close Look at the Meanings of the Words

1. The two words *acupressure* and *acupuncture* start with the same three letters: *acu*. Those three letters mean "at an exact spot." *Pressure* comes from the word *to press*. It means to push down on one area with the thumb or the hand. Acupressure stops the flow of blood and electrical signals to a part of the body. When a muscle has no blood or electricity, it must relax. *Acupuncture* involves very fine needles. These thin sterile needles are inserted into points in the electrical system of the body. They can stop pain. Acupressure and acupuncture are part of Chinese medicine.

2. Several of the elements are named in this story: *oxygen, magnesium, calcium, sodium,* and *potassium.* Do you know the names of other elements?

3. Some parts of the human body are mentioned too: *knee, elbow, bowels, finger, hand, ankle, arm, back, shoulder, armpit, blood,* and *brain.* Do you know others?

4. A *loop* is a circle or another similar shape that returns to the original point. Some letters of the alphabet are written in script (not printed) as loops: *o, e,* and *l,* for example. The small letters *b, d, f, g, h, j, k, p, q, t,* and *y* can be written with loops too. Do you write any capital letters with loops?

Terror in the Train Station

The Central Train Station in Warsaw, Poland, is close to the Palace of Culture. Passengers enter from the street and go down to the trains in the tunnels below ground.

Before You Read the Story

Use these questions as preparation for reading the story. If you need to know the meaning of a word or idiom, check the Words and Idioms List after the story.

1. What does the title of this story tell you?
2. How does it feel to be afraid?
3. Why should a person feel afraid in a train station?

While You Read the Story

Read these questions and look for the answers as you read the story.

1. Who is telling the story?
2. What is the family in the story like?
3. How does the storyteller feel at the beginning, middle, and end of the story?

Terror in the Train Station

1   I came home from school one day in early December 1989. My mother told us of a decision that we all had to make. She had been offered a job with the Peace Corps. For two years we could be in Poland, opening up Central Europe for Peace

5   Corps volunteer work. After a lot of discussing, weighing the pros and cons, and dreaming, we all agreed.

I had heard wonderful stories of Poland: green fields, happy people, beautiful buildings, and wonderful parties. What a dream! I was going to join a country with rich history and a

10   grand future. It was a country to which my family had many ancestral ties.

I had read how the people had voted Communism out. I read about the changes that could be seen everywhere, every day. With free enterprise booming and democracy blooming,

15   how wonderful an experience this could be. I couldn't sleep on the airplane for the whole twenty-hour trip. How could I rest with such visions in my head? I was thirteen, and my sister was fourteen.

The first thing that I noticed about Warsaw was that

20   everything seemed dark. Everything was gray. There were no billboards, no advertising, no color anywhere, just iron bars and gates. The house we lived in was a target for criminals because Americans lived there. It was somewhat of a fortress. We had gates in the front and back, the kind that you "buzz"

25   to let someone through. The walls were thick concrete, with bars on every window. How strange they seemed to a teenaged American boy.

The next thing that I noticed was the people. Happy? Not
even close. They all looked old, tired, worn down, and just
30 plain broken. They seemed to have lost every bit of spirit.
They lived their lives following every rule, without questioning.
They never looked at anyone else; they just kept their heads
down and blended into the crowds. Nothing would happen
to them if they didn't stick out. Nothing bad, nothing good.
35 Nothing at all.

Our problem as Americans was that we did not blend in.
You can tell an American from a mile away. We stick out like
sore thumbs. We walk with the hip-swinging freedom of
walking, not the from-the-knees shuffle of the broken spirited.
40 We held our heads up high and looked into people's eyes
instead of bowing and focusing on our shoes. We smiled at
others whose eyes we happened to meet, smiled out of
interest in life itself; we did not hold our pain on our faces.
We looked like just another American family on tour.

45 Weeks of language and culture classes followed the
arrival of the first group of volunteers. The volunteers and
my family learned together in a high school building in a
small city east of Warsaw, called Torün. We had a great deal
of fun learning about this new country, the people, and the
50 language.

Torün was only three hours from Warsaw by train. The
cost was so low that we took the train home every weekend.
First class was the way to go; a narrow corridor the entire
length of the car made it easy to get in. Sliding glass doors
55 shut off five little rooms, or compartments, each holding six
passengers. They kept the noise out and gave us a sense of
privacy. This was also the only place in all of Poland where
you could truly get a non-smoking room.

One Sunday evening, when we were returning to Torün, our dream turned into a nightmare. We were at Warszawa Centralna, the most convenient train station for us. The train tracks lay about 100 feet below downtown Warsaw. It was necessary to go underground to board the trains. We had been warned to be careful in the dark tunnels of Centralna.

When the Communists left Poland, they did the people no favors. They were told to let all the political prisoners go free. Instead they let everyone go, including the violent criminals. Those who still wished for a life of crime stole cars or broke into houses, hence the bars and gates. Others chose a quicker means; their direct route to finance was right out of others' pockets. Pickpockets and muggers were everywhere, especially in the tunnels of Centralna, where they ruled.

The mistakes that we made that afternoon seem so obvious now. We were told not to speak English in the tunnels. We were also told to always have a woman board a train with us. There was safety in families. There was safety in numbers, three or more. If we followed these rules, then we would not be targets. This day we made every mistake in the book. We were late. We pushed our bags—ten bags for four people—in through the window of the train. We had planned on staying in Torün for two weeks, so we had brought more than usual. Loading through the window seemed the only possible way to get all the stuff on in time. Polish trains are very prompt; we had only about a minute before the horn would blow and the train would leave the station.

90   My mother, my sister, and I hurried on with our hand luggage. Then I was at the window, on the receiving end, while my dad passed the big bags through the window. We completed the task, and I started for the entrance to board with him, alongside my mother.

95   The thugs have a specific method. They wait in the small entrance area of a train. They watch for a rich-looking man. Then they corner him, spray him with Chemical Mace, take everything of value, and jump off the train.

There were a lot of people in the hallway; my dad got to 100 the entrance just as the whistle blew. He was there before we were. He got on alone. And he was attacked. It all happened so fast. I heard my father say, "Get your hands off me!" We tried to hurry to him, but we couldn't move fast because of the crowd in the hallway. I choked on the air of fire that 105 came rushing from the door. The poison Chemical Mace only made everything harder. Other passengers were now running from the toxic air.

Everything went blurry. My face, eyes, nose, and mouth burned. It felt like a pot of boiling water had been poured on 110 me. My nose bled; I couldn't see or even breathe, but I had to get to my dad. My pain was nothing compared to my fear for my father. When I got to my dad, I couldn't make out any details of what had happened. I could see his eyes. They were alive but not normal. He was in shock. I looked at his 115 shirt, and I was shocked too.

There was blood everywhere, coming out of his mouth, on his shirt, on his pants. I thought he had been stabbed with a knife. I couldn't speak. I couldn't ask him. His leg had been broken at the ankle. It was bent in an unnatural way. 120 My mom and I lifted him off the train and set him down.

My sister, Josie, was still on the train. My mother told her to scream as loud as she could, "Don't let the train leave!" It had worked. My sister's screams prevented the train from leaving.

125 Somehow I got the bags off the train by myself. I had so much adrenaline in me I could have done anything—twisted iron, felled Goliath. Sixty-pound suitcases were light as newspapers in my hands as I threw them through the windows and off the train. My mom ran to get help, to call the embassy, and to get the police when the paramedics showed 130 up. I didn't know what to do. Before I could even think of a plan, they were taking my dad away. I told my sister to go with him. Josie was a thin and pretty fourteen-year-old girl. She couldn't stay with the bags and wait for Mom. I was stronger than she was, but I was afraid. We had so much 135 luggage, we were carrying important government documents, and my mom had been gone forever. I was alone, in an underground tunnel with strangers watching me, less than thirty feet from where my dad had fallen. And the bright red on the black cement was my father's blood.

140 I was in terror and terrible pain. The Mace burned, especially my eyes. I started to cry. I was alone in the dark of Warszawa Centralna, where thieves ruled. I was thirteen years old. I was guarding enough baggage to make any thief drool. I cried as quietly as I could, trying to stop shaking 145 with fear. Trying to feel courage. Trying to be brave.

Words and Idioms List

You already know some of these words and idioms. Go through the list. Write a check (✓) next to each of those that you do not know.

Some of these words and idioms may be completely new for you. Find them in the reading. Use the sentences around them to understand what they mean. Note how they are used. These are the words and idioms to learn for this story.

1. _____ **adrenaline** (non-count noun): a body hormone (chemical) that is a response to danger (Adrenaline gives a person strength in times of danger.)

2. _____ **ancestral ties** (plural noun): family history in a place

3. _____ a **billboard** (noun): a large, colorful advertising on the street or road

4. _____ to **bleed** (verb): to have blood flowing from the body as a result of injury (past tense = *bled*)

5. _____ to **blend in** (verb): to seem like everyone else; to fit into a situation naturally

6. _____ **blooming** (adjective): flowering; growing

7. _____ **blurry** (adjective): unclear to the eyes

8. _____ **booming** (adjective): growing fast; increasing

9. _____ **Chemical Mace** (non-count noun, proper noun): a poison gas used by police to stop criminals

10. _____ to **choke** (verb): to cough; to not be able to breathe normally

11. _____ **Communism** (noun): the political system of the former USSR, China, and some other countries

12. _____ a **corridor** (noun): a hallway

13. _____ **crime** (non-count noun): acts that are against the law

14. _____ a **criminal** (noun): a lawbreaker

15. _____ a **direct route** (idiom): a straight way to a goal

16. _____ to **drool** (verb): to salivate; to have one's appetite become sharp; to desire something greatly

17. _____ **finance** (non-count noun): money matters

18. _____ **free enterprise** (non-count noun): a marketing system that allows competition

19. _____ **Goliath** (proper name): the giant who was killed by the boy David in a Bible story

20. _____ a **mugger** (noun): a person who attacks another to rob him or her

21. _____ a **paramedic** (noun): a person who has some training in taking care of hurt people (A paramedic usually arrives in an ambulance.)

22. _____ to **pickpocket** (noun): a person who steals from others' pockets

23. _____ **poison** (non-count noun): a substance that can hurt a person; a toxin

24. _____ **privacy** (non-count noun): a feeling of being alone

25. _____ **prompt** (adjective): on time

26. _____ **pros and cons** (idiom): positive and negative aspects

27. _____ to **shuffle** (verb): to move one's feet without lifting them from the ground

28. _____ **spirit** (non-count noun): soul; sense of being; sense of joy

29. _____ to **stab** (verb): to push a knife into

30. _____ to **stick out** (verb): to be obvious

31. _____ a **target** (noun): a mark to be attacked; a focus

32. _____ a **thug** (noun): a criminal; a thief

33. _____ **violent** (adjective): physically forceful; cruel; fierce; powerful

34. _____ a **volunteer** (noun): a person who works without pay

After You Have Read the Story

Do you have the answers to the questions from "While You Read the Story"? Talk about the answers with your classmates.

Understanding Sequence

In the blank in front of each phrase, write 2–11 to show that you know the order of the story.

    a. _____ ambulance and paramedics arriving

    b. _____ left alone guarding the luggage and waiting for mother to return

    c. _____ moving to Poland

    d. _____ mother going for help and leaving children with the father

    e. __1__ hearing about the possibility of going to Poland

    f. _____ taking the train every weekend home to Warsaw

    g. _____ helping the father off the train

    h. _____ returning to Torün on the train late one Sunday

    i. _____ sister going off to the hospital with the father

    j. _____ the father being attacked by muggers

    k. _____ deciding as a family to go overseas

Answering Questions About the Story

Read these questions, think about the answers, and then discuss the answers with your classmates.

1. How long would the family be in Poland?
2. Why had the boy heard about Poland?
3. Why were the train stations dangerous?
4. Why are Americans easy to identify?
5. How far below ground were the train tracks in Warsaw?
6. What do violent criminals do?

7. Why were there iron bars and gates on every house?

8. Why were there so many pickpockets and muggers around the train station?

9. How did the paramedics know about the attack?

10. What makes first-class train travel nice?

Drawing Conclusions from the Story

Which of these statements are probably true, from the information in the story? Write *true* or *false* in the blank in front of each sentence.

1. _____ There were reasons for the family to return to their home in Warsaw frequently.

2. _____ Life in Poland had been very hard under the rule of Communism.

3. _____ There was a lot of advertising under Communist rule.

4. _____ Thieves never attacked foreigners.

5. _____ It is a long way from the boy's home to Poland.

6. _____ There was a big school in Torün.

7. _____ Six people could ride in the compartments of one train car.

8. _____ Warszawa Centralna was the train station in Torün.

9. _____ Chemical Mace is dangerous to eyes.

10. _____ The boy's father was stabbed.

Finding the Meaning in Context

A. Which meaning is closest to the underlined word or words? Circle *a*, *b*, *c*, or *d*.

1. I began to <u>cough</u> because of the Chemical Mace.

   a. call   c. bleed

   b. choke   d. stab

2. I was looking out the window, and everything was clear. Then suddenly everything was <u>unclear</u>.

   a. poison
            c. booming

   b. blooming
          d. blurry

3. There was a large <u>advertisement</u> about a new movie on the street.

   a. mugger
            c. billboard

   b. finance
           d. corridor

4. There are many young <u>lawbreakers</u> in the prison.

   a. muggers
           c. paramedics

   b. pickpockets
       d. criminals

5. I ran down the <u>hallway</u> of the school, looking for a door to the street.

   a. corridor
           c. target

   b. room
            d. compartment

B. Find the word in this list that completes each sentence and write the correct form of it in the blank.

shuffle	drool	stab	bleed
bloom	boom	mug	choke

1. When I think of lemons or pickles, I usually _____ .

2. The man used his knife to _____ a big juicy apple and cut it up to eat.

3. After a day of rain and two days of bright sunshine, the tulips started to _____ .

4. One criminal attacked another. It was unusual for one lawbreaker to _____ another.

5. I fell and hurt my knee. It began to _____ , so I needed to get a bandage.

6. The old man doesn't walk with confidence. Instead, he

   _____ .

7. The child put a big piece of candy in her mouth, and soon she couldn't

   breathe. She had begun to _____ .

8. The business started out slowly, but suddenly, after two months, it

   _____ .

Matching New Words and Meanings

A. Draw a line between the two words or phrases with similar meanings.

1. doctor's assistants		a. on time
2. bag		b. hurry
3. toxic		c. suitcase
4. entrance		d. mugger
5. baggage		e. poison
6. move fast		f. terror
7. prompt		g. corridor
8. thief		h. door
9. fear		i. paramedics
10. hallway		j. luggage

B. Find the words and phrases in the two columns above that complete the sentences and write the correct form of each one in the blanks.

1. When someone is not late, that person is _____ or

   _____ .

2. Both _____ and _____ refer to fast

   action.

3. Both _____ and _____ mean all the

   things that a traveler carries with him.

4. A _____ and a _____ refer to single examples of the words in #3.

5. Both a _____ and a _____ are criminals.

6. Both a _____ and a _____ are long, narrow rooms with doors to other rooms.

7. A _____ and a _____ both mean a way into a room or place.

8. _____ and _____ refer to dangerous substances (gases or liquids).

9. The feeling of being afraid is either _____ or

   _____ .

10. _____ and _____ are both people who help others in emergencies.

Practicing with Idioms

Find the idiom in this list that means the same or almost the same as the underlined words and use the correct form of it to complete each sentence. Note that some words (for example, [*someone*]) can be replaced with other words and might be in another position in the sentence.

to weigh the pros and cons	to stick out
to blend in	to get to [someone]
to do [someone] no favors	to open [something] up
to corner [someone]	to let [someone] go free
to hold [one's] head up high	to vote [someone] out
to let [someone] through	to be the way to go

1. The people chose a new president and <u>decided against</u> the old government.

   The people chose a new president and _____ the old government.

2. Flying <u>is the preferred means of travel</u>.

   Flying _____ .

3. The leaders <u>opened the prison doors</u> for all prisoners.

   The leaders _____ the prisoners _____ .

4. We <u>talked about the positive and negative parts of the idea</u> before we decided.

   We _____ before we decided.

5. A single red car <u>is obvious among</u> many black cars.

   A single red car _____ among many black cars.

6. On the other hand, a foreign car that is black will <u>not be noticed</u>.

   On the other hand, a foreign car that is black will _____ among many black cars.

7. The young soldiers always <u>walk with pride</u>.

   The young soldiers always _____ .

8. The man who hired me <u>didn't really help me much</u>.

   The man who hired me _____ .

9. The mystery would still be unsolved if the detective hadn't <u>started to investigate</u> it.

   The mystery would still be unsolved if the detective hadn't

   _____ it.

10. Please <u>allow</u> this person <u>to pass to the other side of the crowd</u>.

    Please _____ this person _____ .

11. May I make a phone call? I need <u>to reach</u> a friend before nine o'clock.

    May I make a phone call? I need _____ a friend before nine o'clock.

12. The newspaper reporter <u>stopped</u> the famous man and asked him questions <u>before the man could leave</u>.

The newspaper reporter _____ the famous man and asked him questions.

Exploring the Ideas

Think about these questions. Talk about your opinions with your classmates.

1. Is it good to blend in when you are in a new country?
2. Why is first class "the way to go?"
3. How can you tell a person whose spirit is broken?
4. What was the thieves' method for robbing train travelers? What do you think of this method?
5. How did the boy know that his father was in shock?
6. Why was the mother afraid that the train would leave? How did the family stop the train from leaving?
7. What gave the boy more strength than usual?
8. How did they know that the father's leg was broken?
9. How did they get help? (Name two ways.)
10. Why were the boy's eyes blurry?

Making Inferences

Read the numbered sentence. Then read the sentences under it. Which ones are true because the numbered sentence is true? Circle the letter in front of each true statement.

1. Some criminals chose a quicker means, a direct route to finance right out of others' pockets.
   a. A direct route to finance is robbing others.
   b. A person who takes money from another person is a criminal.
   c. Taking someone else's money is a fast way to get your hands on some money.
   d. All the freed criminals were thieves.

2. We were going to a country with a rich history and a grand future.

   a. There is no history in Poland.

   b. Life in Poland was getting better.

   c. Many things in Poland were changing.

   d. The reason we were going was to learn the history.

3. Poland is a country to which my family has many ancestral ties.

   a. The family has relatives in Poland.

   b. The family is tied to the country.

   c. The family's name is probably English.

   d. The name of the country is Polish.

4. We had a great deal of fun learning about this new country, the people, and the language.

   a. It is fun to learn new things.

   b. The school for the Peace Corps people was quite good.

   c. They enjoyed learning about Poland.

   d. The Polish language is interesting.

5. We had been warned to be careful in the dark tunnels of Centralna.

   a. There had been trouble with other foreigners and thieves there.

   b. The dark tunnels were dangerous places.

   c. Someone had told them how to act in the tunnels.

   d. They were usually careful in the train station.

Finding the Main Ideas

Read all these titles. Some of them are possible titles for this story. Draw a line between each of those titles and *Appropriate*. Others are not appropriate titles. Read the reasons that some are not appropriate, and draw a line between each of those titles and the reason it was not appropriate.

Titles	Reasons
1. A Boy and His Sister	
2. An Adventure in a Foreign Country	APPROPRIATE
3. Nightmare in Centralna	
4. Muggers and Pickpockets Get My Father	too broad
5. Train Station Mistakes	
6. Finding Something Red on the Cement	tells the whole story
7. Poland	
8. The Day My Father Was Beaten Up in the Train Station	too narrow
9. In the Dark Tunnels of the Train Station	

Reading for Details

A. Find the answers to these questions in the story.

1. When does the story begin?
2. Where is Poland?
3. How old was the boy? His sister?
4. How long did the trip from home to Poland take?
5. What kind of gate did the house have?
6. Who is telling the story?
7. How can you tell an American from a Pole?
8. What is Toruń?
9. What is Warszawa Centralna?
10. What poison was used?

B. Find this information in the story:

1. What was booming?
2. What were the walls made of?
3. Who stick out like sore thumbs?
4. How far is Torün from Warsaw?
5. How many people can sit in one compartment on a train?
6. Who ruled the tunnels of Centralna?
7. How many bags did the family have that day?
8. Where in Poland could you get a non-smoking room in 1990?
9. What did the family go to Torün to learn?
10. How far from the train door did the boy have to wait with the baggage?

Taking a Close Look at the Meanings of the Words

1. Any man who is very large and strong compared to others might be called *Goliath*. There is a story about a young shepherd boy, David, who became a hero. The giant Goliath was killing many people. He even threatened the young shepherd. When the giant was about to kill David, David took a stone from the ground and used a slingshot (a simple weapon made of a string of leather) to kill the evil man. The stone kit the giant's head and killed him. (David caused Goliath to fall. David felled Goliath.)

2. *Adrenaline* is the name of one body chemical. Adrenaline is a response to danger. It makes a person stronger and more alert. Other *hormones* cause other kinds of human responses. For example, there is a hormone that makes men's beards grow. It is called *testosterone*. The hormone that women have is called *estrogen*.

3. *Communism* and *free enterprise* are two different systems. In theory, where there is Communism, every person has a job and gets what food and money he or she needs to live. In a free enterprise system, people can choose to try to work harder to earn more. People can also fail in business and lose everything.

Aunt Agnes's Wedding Ring

Agnes's wedding day was the happiest day of her life.

Before You Read the Story

Use these questions as preparation for reading the story. If you need to know the meaning of a word or idiom, check the Words and Idioms List after the story. In fact, you might want to check the list before you read the story.

1. What do you know just from the title?

2. What do you know about Agnes just from the title?

3. What words do you know about weddings and marriages? Work with your classmates to make a list of the words you know in this area.

While You Read the Story

Read these questions and look for the answers as you read the story.

1. What kind of person is Agnes?

2. How do we know that she is a hard worker?

3. What does Agnes always do on Mondays?

4. Who is telling this story?

5. What do we learn from this story about how much people don't change?

6. What made the ring so precious to Agnes?

7. Think about the title of this story. Circle the ideas and words in the following list that you expect to be in the story.

ring	job	wife	husband
family	children	nail	to be born
books	baby	sister	daughter
tourists	bakery	bath	laundry
church	farm	map	to be married
kitchen	marriage	son	plumber
house	farmer	cousin	

Aunt Agnes's Wedding Ring

1   Agnes met Tony at a community picnic. He was tall and
handsome, and he had a good job. He worked as a pipe fitter
at the paper mill in town. On the side, Tony worked as a
plumber. He fixed the leaky faucets and plugged drain pipes
5   of people's homes. He made good money because the people
in town knew that Tony was a good honest worker. To Agnes,
Tony looked like the kind of man a woman could marry and
live with happily.

         Agnes had been only fifteen when she came from the
10   farm in Lena to help her older sister Anna. Anna's husband,
my grandfather, had a grocery business in town. They had
many people working for them in the store. Anna had to help
in the store, to keep the workers on the job. So Agnes came
to help with the children. After a year, another cousin came
15   from Iron River to help at the house. That's when Agnes got
a job at the bakery in town. She learned how to make bread
and all kinds of fancy cakes and cookies. Everyone loved
Agnes, especially Tony. Agnes was easy to love because she
was so pretty and so much fun. She was also a very good
20   cook. Agnes was the kind of woman a man could marry and
live with happily.

         About a year later, Tony asked Agnes to marry him. Tony
bought a house on the main street of town and fixed it up.
He painted it and put in nice carpeting. The house had two
25   stories. There was a kitchen, dining room, living room, and
front porch on the first floor. Upstairs, there were three large
bedrooms, a bathroom, and an attic storage place. In the
basement, there was a place for the car, a workshop for Tony's
plumbing tools, and a neat laundry room with a washing

30 machine, a long table, and two big lead sinks. It was a comfortable house. When Tony and Agnes got married, they moved in. Nothing could mar their happiness.

The catastrophe happened a week after their marriage, on a Monday morning. Agnes lost her wedding ring. Tony
35 had saved all his extra money for nearly a year to buy Agnes the gold band with seven little diamonds in it. And Agnes lost it. She remembered having it in the morning as she was taking the dirty clothes downstairs to the basement to wash them in her new washing machine. However, at noon, she no
40 longer had the ring on her finger.

Agnes was beyond comfort, but at first she couldn't even tell Tony. She told her sister, and Agnes and Anna searched the house from top to bottom, but the ring was nowhere to be found. When Agnes told Tony, he took the pipes in the
45 laundry room apart, in case the ring had fallen into one of the drains. However, the ring was gone. Agnes found a simple silver band to wear in place of the precious wedding ring Tony had given her on their wedding day. Every day she saw that silver band. Every day she thought about her lost wedding ring.

50 The years passed, and their children were born. First came three daughters. Joan was their first, and then Delores was born. A few years later Maureen was born, and then they had a son, Roger. Their marriage was a happy one, but Agnes never stopped looking for her wedding ring.

55 The children grew up and went to college, and Agnes and Tony were happy and proud of their family. On their thirtieth wedding anniversary, Tony surprised Agnes with a special gift. It was a gold wedding ring with seven little diamonds. It was just like the one he had given her on their wedding
60 day thirty years before. Agnes thought for a moment that

Tony had found the lost ring, but then she realized that he had bought her a new one. She was very happy, because a beautiful wedding ring meant a lot to her.

65 A few days later, on Monday morning, Agnes picked up the basket of dirty clothes to go downstairs to her laundry room. She had a new automatic washing machine now. However, she still liked to wash some things by hand in the big lead sinks. She put the black rubber plug into one sink and
70 turned on the faucet. She was feeling the temperature of the water as she prepared to wash a white sweater by hand. She saw

how the diamonds of the new wedding ring sparkled in the water. She gently took the ring off her finger. She wasn't
75 going to lose this ring! She looked up at the wooden rafters above her washing machine. She wanted to find a nail on which to put her new ring. And there she saw a nail. But there was something on it! There hung her first wedding ring, which she had put there to be safe, thirty years before.

Words and Idioms List

You already know some of these words and idioms. Go through the list. Write a check (✔) next to each of those that you do not know.

Some of these words and idioms may be completely new for you. Find them in the reading. Use the sentences around them to understand what they mean. Note how they are used. These are the words and idioms to learn for this story.

1. _____   an **attic** (noun): an empty area at the top of a house, used for storing things

2. _____ a **basement** (noun): an area, like a room, under a house where storage rooms and workrooms are often made

3. _____ to **be beyond comfort** (idiom): to be so sad as to be unable to accept comfort

4. _____ a **catastrophe** (noun): a disaster; a sad or terrible event

5. _____ a **drain** (noun): an open pipe through which water usually flows or can flow from top to bottom (idiom) thoroughly

6. _____ to **help at the house** (idiom): to do housework and take care of children

7. _____ to **keep workers on the job** (idiom): to supervise workers

8. _____ **lead** (non-count noun): the name of a heavy metal (chemical symbol = *Pb*)

9. _____ a **leaky faucet** (idiom): a water tap that cannot turn off all the way, so water escapes from it

10. _____ to **mar** (verb): to spoil; to blemish

11. _____ **nowhere to be found** (idiom): lost; unable to be located

12. _____ a **pipe fitter** (noun): a skilled worker who works with pipes and valves in water systems in a factory or mill

13. _____ a **plug** (noun): a drain stopper; a rubber or plastic piece that fits into the top of a drain so that water cannot flow out

14. _____ a **plugged drain** (idiom): a pipe through which water cannot flow because something (such as roots, food, or grease) stops the water

15. _____ a **plumber** (noun): a skilled worker who works with pipes, valves, water, and sewer systems

16. _____ **precious** (adjective): very valuable

17. _____ to **think for a moment** (idiom): to stop to consider, or to be mistaken in one's understanding

18. _____ to **wash some things by hand** (idiom): to clean some special items of clothing without using a washing machine

19. _____ a **wooden rafter** (noun): a piece of wood that is used with others just like it to support a floor above it; part of an unfinished ceiling

After You Have Read the Story

Do you have the answers to the questions from "While You Read the Story"? Talk about the answers with your classmates.

Understanding Sequence

In the blank in front of each sentence, write 2–12 to show that you know the order of the story.

a. _____ Thirty years passed.

b. _____ They had four children who grew up and went away to college.

c. __1__ Agnes met Tony at a community picnic.

d. _____ Tony bought a house and fixed it up.

e. _____ Agnes and Tony got married.

f. _____ She and her sister searched the house, but they could not find it.

g. _____ Agnes found her first ring when she looked for a safe place to put her second ring.

h. _____ Tony saved all his extra money for a year to buy a special wedding ring.

i. _____ For their thirtieth wedding anniversary, Tony bought Agnes a wedding ring just like the first one.

j. _____ Agnes put a simple silver ring on her finger in place of the beautiful wedding band.

k. _____ Agnes lost her wedding ring the week after their marriage.

l. _____ Tony fell in love and started to save money.

Answering Questions About the Story

Read these questions, think about the answers, and then discuss the answers with your classmates.

1. How did Agnes and Tony meet?
2. How old was Agnes when she came to town from the farm?
3. About how old was Agnes when she got married?
4. What did Tony look like when he was a young man?
5. How much education do you think Agnes had?
6. Where did Anna's cousins live? (Name two places.)
7. What rooms did they have upstairs in their house?
8. When did the catastrophe happen?
9. What marred their happiness?
10. What did the silver band make Agnes think about? Why did she wear it?

Drawing Conclusions from the Story

Which of these statements are probably true, from the information in the story? Write *true* or *false* in the blank in front of each sentence.

1. _____ Agnes wanted to stay on the farm.

2. _____ Tony liked to eat good food.

3. _____ Anna needed help with her business and her family.

4. _____ Agnes didn't like her wedding ring.

5. _____ Tony didn't want to buy a diamond wedding ring for Agnes.

6. _____ People who work in a bakery make cakes and cookies.

7. _____ A person who works in a grocery store sells cakes and cookies.

8. _____ There were often community picnics in the town.

9. _____ The houses on the main street were the best houses in town.

10. _____ A house needs to have a kitchen and a bathroom.

Finding the Meaning in Context

Which meaning is closest to the underlined word or words? Circle *a, b, c,* or *d.*

1. Losing the wedding ring was <u>a disaster</u> for Agnes.
   - a. a catastrophe
   - b. an attic
   - c. a plug
   - d. a wonderful thing

2. Agnes's happiness was <u>spoiled</u> by the loss of her ring.
   - a. precious
   - b. plugged
   - c. marred
   - d. beyond comfort

3. In the <u>area under the roof</u>, we keep boxes of the children's things.
   - a. basement
   - b. bedroom
   - c. kitchen
   - d. attic

4. The water isn't flowing out of the bathtub fast enough. It must be <u>stopped</u> up.
   - a. drained
   - b. plugged
   - c. fitted
   - d. washed

5. The diamond ring was quite <u>valuable</u>.
   - a. leaky
   - b. wooden
   - c. precious
   - d. spoiled

6. Because the faucet is <u>dripping water</u>, we need to call for help.
   - a. leaky
   - b. wooden
   - c. precious
   - d. marred

7. Let's call a <u>worker who is skilled in repairing faucets and water pipes</u>.
   - a. baker
   - b. worker
   - c. plumber
   - d. husband

8. The ceiling of the basement used to be <u>long wooden pieces</u>, but now it is covered with white squares.

   a. attics   c. drains

   b. faucets   d. rafters

9. Water flows out of the laundry room through a <u>special pipe</u>.

   a. faucet   c. plug

   b. drain   d. catastrophe

10. Many pipes used to be made of <u>a very heavy metal</u>.

   a. rubber   c. wood

   b. lead   d. diamonds

Matching New Words and Meanings

A. Draw a line between the two words or phrases with similar meanings.

1. husband		a.	silver
2. cakes		b.	plumber
3. mill		c.	laundry
4. bakery		c.	ring
5. aunt		d.	grocery
6. gold		e.	wife
7. attic		f.	daughter
8. band		g.	plugged
9. pipe fitter		h.	basement
10. leaky		i.	cousin
11. dirty clothes		j.	cookies
12. son		k.	factory

B. Find the words and phrases in the two columns above that complete the sentences and write the correct form of each one in the blanks.

1. Both a _____ and a _____ work with water systems.

2. The two things that are circles of metal are a _____
   and a _____ .

3. One's children are either _____ or _____ .

4. A _____ and his _____ are a married
   couple.

5. Both _____ and _____ go into the
   washing machine.

6. Products like paper are made in a _____ or a
   _____ .

7. People who are members of one's family are an _____
   and a _____ .

8. People can buy food at a _____ and a
   _____ .

9. _____ and _____ are two precious
   metals.

10. A baker makes _____ and _____ .

11. The _____ and the _____ are the top
    and bottom of a house.

12. A faucet or a pipe can be _____ or _____ .
    Both are plumbing problems.

Practicing with Idioms

Find the idiom in this list that means the same or almost the same as the underlined word or words and use the correct form of it to complete each sentence. Note that some words (for example, [*something*]) can be replaced with other words and might be in another position in the sentence.

to make good money	to keep [someone] on the job
from top to bottom	to help out at the house
to be proud of something	to work on the side
to wash [something] by hand	to think [something] for a moment
to be beyond comfort	nowhere to be found

1. You should <u>not wash</u> a beautiful sweater <u>in a washing machine</u>.

   You should _____ a beautiful sweater _____ .

2. Why do some people look for different jobs when they <u>are earning a lot at a job</u> already?

   Why do some people look for different jobs when they

   _____ already?

3. She is a teacher, but she <u>has another job</u> as a baker.

   She is a teacher, but she _____ as a baker.

4. A supervisor has to <u>make sure</u> that all the workers <u>are working well</u>.

   A supervisor has to _____ that all the workers

   _____ .

5. The ring was <u>lost</u>.

   The ring was _____ .

6. On the farm there were six men to work in the fields but there was no one <u>to assist the farmer's wife</u>.

   On the farm there were six men to work in the fields but there was

   no one _____ .

7. When Agnes realized that the wedding ring was gone, she <u>was very sad</u>.

   When Agnes realized that the wedding ring was gone, she

   _____ .

8. Agnes searched <u>every part of</u> the house.

   Agnes searched the house _____ .

9. I looked outside, and <u>at first I thought</u> that it was raining.

   I looked outside, and I _____ that it was raining.

10. They had <u>good feelings about</u> their family.

    They _____ their family.

Exploring the Ideas

Think about these questions. Talk about your opinions with your classmates.

1. Was Agnes careless with the ring?
2. Why do you think Agnes forgot about where she had put the wedding ring?
3. What could Agnes have been thinking about when she took off her first wedding ring?
4. Why did Tony take the pipes in the laundry room apart?
5. What do you think of Tony's gift to Agnes on their thirtieth wedding anniversary?
6. What does a wedding ring mean to most people?
7. What do most people have in their basements?
8. What is an attic for?
9. Why didn't Agnes tell her husband about the lost ring immediately?
10. What words do you know to describe diamonds?

Making Inferences

Read the numbered sentence. Then read the sentences under it. Which ones are true because the numbered sentence is true? Circle the letter in front of each true statement.

1. Anna had to help in the store, to keep the workers on the job.
   a. Anna didn't trust the workers to do a good job.
   b. The workers were not good honest workers.
   c. Someone had to watch the workers in the store.
   d. The workers in the store sometimes took food home.
   e. There were no workers in the store.

2. Tony bought a house on the main street of town and fixed it up.
   a. Tony was a good worker.
   b. There were houses on the main street of town for sale.
   c. Tony bought a new house.
   d. The house that Tony bought needed some repairs.
   e. Tony was getting ready to ask Agnes to marry him.

3. Tony took the pipes of the laundry room apart, in case the ring had fallen into one of the drains.
   a. Tony knew how to fix pipes.
   b. He thought that the ring had fallen down a drain.
   c. Agnes was in the laundry room when she lost her ring.
   d. There were a lot of pipes in the laundry room.

4. Agnes found a simple silver band to wear in place of the precious wedding ring that Tony had given her on their wedding day.
   a. Agnes could not afford to buy a new wedding ring.
   b. Agnes pretended that her wedding ring was silver.
   c. Agnes wasn't an honest person.
   d. Agnes wanted everyone to know that she was married.
   e. Agnes loved her first wedding ring.

5. Agnes looked up at the wooden rafters above the washing machine for a nail on which to put her ring.

    a. Agnes was looking for a safe place to put her ring.

    b. There was no regular ceiling in the laundry room.

    c. There were nails in the ceiling.

    d. A nail in a rafter is a safe place to put a ring.

Finding the Main Ideas

Write *MI* in front of each main idea and *SI* in front of each supporting idea.

1. _____ Agnes lost her wedding ring.

2. _____ Agnes had a sister.

3. _____ Tony enjoyed picnics.

4. _____ Tony and Agnes got married.

5. _____ They had four children.

6. _____ Tony bought a new ring for Agnes on their thirtieth wedding anniversary.

7. _____ Agnes had a nice laundry room with a new washing machine.

8. _____ Tony worked as a plumber on the side.

9. _____ Agnes and Tony owned their own home.

10. _____ Agnes found her wedding ring where she had put it.

Reading for Details

Find the answers to these questions in the story.

1. How old was Agnes when she went to work at the bakery?

2. How long did it take Tony to fix up the house?

3. How long did Tony save his extra money to buy the first wedding ring with seven diamonds?

4. Where did Tony work?

5. What was his job there?

6. What did he do on the side?

7. How did he earn extra money?

8. Who was Anna?

9. Where was the farm?

10. What were the rooms in Tony's house?

11. What was in the laundry room?

12. Why did Tony need a workshop?

13. How many children did they have?

14. How did Agnes find her ring?

Taking a Close Look at the Meanings of the Words

1. Not every house has a basement and an attic. In cold climates, a basement is necessary because of the need for heat. The word *base* means "foundation." A furnace is usually in the basement, and the pipes (or ducts) that carry heat to the rest of the house start at the furnace. An attic is usually right under the roof. A house must have a pitched roof to have an attic. A pitched roof is higher in the middle so rain and snow will fall off it.

2. A wedding is a reason for a celebration. There is a wedding ceremony, sometimes at a church. A wedding anniversary is another reason for celebration. Married couples often have a big party on their tenth, twenty-fifth, thirtieth, and fiftieth wedding anniversaries.

Baby Polish

Meeting the language barrier was a challenge in Kraków. How could young tourists communicate without a common language? Or is getting the message across the most important part of communication?

Before You Read the Story

Use these questions as preparation for reading the story. If you need to know the meaning of a word or idiom, check the Words and Idioms List after the story.

1. What does the title tell you?

2. How many words do you know about the topic of traveling and being a tourist? Make a list of these words with your classmates.

While You Read the Story

Read these questions and look for the answers as you read the story.

1. Why was language sure to be a problem?

2. What is more important, to be correct or for other people to understand you? Why?

3. Why did the Polish people laugh at the Americans?

4. Think about the title of this story. What will it be about? Circle the ideas and words that you expect to be in a story with this title.

souvenir	health	school	language
magazine	tourist	country	travel
translate	police	explore	museum
continent	family	kitchen	bathroom
restaurant	map	drive	mystery
separate	bed	visit	car

5. Who is telling this story?

6. Who are the four friends? Why are they unusual?

7. How would Louise, Stephanie, or Susan have told the story? How would Jean's father have told the story?

Baby Polish

1   We four friends were teachers, living and working in Istanbul. Summer was coming, and there was a chance to travel. Where should we go? Louise and Stephanie decided to go to a language school in Switzerland to study French.

5   Susan wanted to go to Germany, to visit some relatives and brush up on German. I was the fourth one. I wanted to see some of Europe and then fly home to the United States to visit my family. The three weeks between the end of our classes and the beginning of the language school in Switzerland was

10   a chance to see Eastern and Central Europe. It was the time before the great changes in Europe. The Iron Curtain still separated the continent. We were brave young people. We were willing to travel to places where most tourists did not go.

      We planned to drive through the Balkan countries to

15   Hungary, Czechoslovakia, Poland, East Germany, to East Berlin and then West Berlin. We would explore the divided city and then go to West Germany, Luxembourg, France, and Switzerland. We planned every detail of our trip. We would stop at tourism offices in train stations to find a family to stay

20   with. We would visit museums, buy souvenirs, and drive on. We even decided which languages we would speak. In Turkey and the Balkans, we would speak Turkish. We would use English if possible, then French or German. And our plan worked, until we got to the south of Poland.

25   We entered Poland late one afternoon. We were hungry, so we stopped at a roadside restaurant. None of our languages worked there, so I ordered bread, butter, cheese, and beer— in Polish. I remembered a few things in Polish from my childhood. In Kraków, as usual, we went to the tourist office

30   at the train station. We found a family that had room for four tourists. With the address card, we drove to the house. The woman of the family greeted us, but it soon became obvious that she knew no foreign languages. She showed us into a large, clean room. However, there were no beds in it, only
35   mystery furniture. She shut the door, and we were alone. Louise asked where the bathroom was. None of us knew. So the other three sent me to the kitchen to find out. The experience in the restaurant had impressed them. I could speak Polish to the lady of the house.

40   In the kitchen I tried every word I could think of: water closet, bathroom, toilet. None of them worked. So I thought and then said something that my grandmother said to us children. It had some relationship to bathrooms. The woman looked at me and made me say it again. She called her husband
45   into the kitchen and made me say it again. They burst into laughter and took me to the water closet. They also showed me the banyo, or shower room, with a flash heater for hot water. I went back to the large room and my three friends, pleased with success.

50   We went out to dinner and a concert. We returned at a good time for showers and going to sleep. We could not, however, figure out the flash heater. This device for heating water was quite different from the ones in Turkey. So Louise, Stephanie, and Susan sent me back to the kitchen for help.
55   This time, I tried acting out taking a shower. The family did not understand, so I tried to think of something in Polish. I remembered something my grandmother said when she put a dirty grandchild into the bathtub. And I said it. This time, the family called their neighbors in. They made me repeat
60   my Polish sentence again and again, then looked at one

another and burst into laughter. Then the man of the family went with me to the shower room and lit the flash heater.

After we showered, we tried to figure out how to turn the mystery furniture into four beds. I went back to the kitchen

65 for help. I didn't try to act out going to sleep. The kitchen was full of people from the neighborhood. So I thought of something in Polish about going to bed. Again and again I said the Polish

70 sentence. The people in the kitchen laughed until they cried. However, the

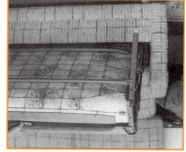

woman and two of her friends went to the big room. They pushed and pulled at the furniture, moving this part and that until the mystery furniture became four beds. And their four

75 American tourists went to sleep.

Ten days later, I was home in Wisconsin. My father, whose native language is Polish, asked how we managed in Poland. I said, "I used my Polish." He said, "You don't know any Polish." I told him the whole story. He stared at me in

80 disbelief. And then he burst into laughter. "Jeanne," he choked out between guffaws, "you were talking baby Polish! 'Do you gotta go tinkle?' "

Words and Idioms List

You already know some of these words and idioms. Go through the list. Write a check (✓) next to each of those that you do not know.

Some of these words and idioms may be completely new for you. Find them in the reading. Use the sentences around them to understand what they mean. Note how they are used. These are the words and idioms to learn for this story.

1. _____ to **act out** (idiom): to pantomime; to show by gestures and actions

2. _____ **baby** (adjective): made simple as for a baby; simple; small

3. _____ the **Balkans** (plural noun): the countries of Southeastern Europe: Slovenia, Croatia, Bosnia and Herzegovina, Yugoslavia, Albania, Macedonia, Bulgaria, Romania, and Greece

4. _____ to **brush up on** (idiom): to practice or improve

5. _____ to **burst into laughter** (idiom): to begin to laugh suddenly

6. _____ a **chance** (noun): an opportunity; free time to use for a purpose

7. _____ to **choke something out** (idiom): to say something while laughing or crying

8. _____ a **continent** (noun): a large land mass (The seven continents are Africa, Antarctica, Asia, Australia, Europe, North America, and South America.)

9. _____ a **device** (noun): a tool or simple machine that has a single purpose

10. _____ **Do you gotta go tinkle?** (idiom, baby talk): Do you need to use a toilet or urinate?

11. _____ to **explore** (verb): to look around; to investigate; to try to get to know

12. _____ a **flash heater** (noun): a box, usually on a wall, through which water pipes run and in which gas flames heat the water in the thin pipes for a kitchen, bath, or laundry

13. _____ to **greet** (verb): to welcome; to say hello

14. _____ a **guffaw** (noun): a big laugh; a laugh that makes the whole body shake

15. _____ to **impress someone** (verb): to do something positive to gain someone's approval; to influence

16. _____ to **manage** (verb): to be successful; to arrange a situation so that one can work in it

17. _____ **mystery furniture** (idiom): furniture that looks unusual or unfamiliar, not ordinary pieces like chairs and tables

18. _____ **roadside** (adjective): said of a building along the side of the road, not in the city

19. _____ a **souvenir** (noun): an object that one buys to remember a place; a memento

20. _____ to **stare in disbelief** (idiom): to look at in shock and surprise

21. _____ a **water closet** (noun): a separate room that contains only a toilet (a commode)

After You Have Read the Story

Do you have the answers to the questions from "While You Read the Story"? Talk about the answers with your classmates.

Understanding Sequence

In the blank in front of each sentence, write 2–10 to show that you know the order of the story.

a. _____ The four tourists traveled through Czechoslovakia and Hungary.

b. _____ They left Istanbul.

c. ___1___ Four friends decided to take a trip behind the Iron Curtain.

d. _____ They found that the people in Kraków didn't speak any foreign languages.

e. _____ They entered Poland.

f. _____ The Americans traveled through the Balkans.

g. _____ They went to the train station in Kraków.

h. _____ The four travelers were successful in Poland.

i. _____ Jean used sentences in Polish from her childhood.

j. _____ They ate at a roadside restaurant in Poland.

Answering Questions About the Story

Read these questions, think about the answers, and then discuss the answers with your classmates.

1. How long did the four friends have to travel?

2. In what country is Istanbul?

3. How did the four friends travel?

4. How did Jean get to Wisconsin?

5. Where is Kraków?

6. What did the four friends want to see? Why?

7. What were their names?

8. Which continent were they traveling around?

9. What did they plan to see in every main city?

10. What did the four tourists do for fun on their first night in Kraków?

Drawing Conclusions from the Reading

Answer these questions with your own ideas.

1. Why were the tourism offices in the train stations of Eastern and Central Europe?

2. At a restaurant you ate "mystery meat." What does that expression mean?

3. Why do you think the four travelers ate only bread, butter, and cheese at the roadside restaurant?

4. The Iron Curtain separated the continent of Europe into two parts. What were these two parts?

5. Why didn't many tourists go to Eastern and Central Europe?

6. Why weren't there many tourist hotels in Eastern and Central Europe?

7. Why is a flash heater a good idea?

8. Why were they probably interested in seeing Berlin?

9. From where did Jean probably fly to the United States?

10. How do we know that these four young people wanted to learn languages?

11. How can a visitor to a city find the train station?

12. Why did Jean know some Polish words and a few Polish sentences?

13. Which of these titles could be good titles for the story?

   a. A Trip Behind the Iron Curtain

   b. Communication Over Perfect Grammar

   c. The Train Stations of Eastern and Central Europe

   d. In the Kitchens of Kraków

Finding the Meaning in Context

Find the word or phrase in this list that means the same or almost the same as the underlined word or words and use the correct form of it to complete each sentence.

continent	chance	explore	souvenirs
water	closet	flash heater	acting out
disbelief	manage	impress	greet
burst	stare	choke out	

1. Louise showed by <u>picking up an empty glass and putting it to her mouth</u> that she wanted something to drink.

   Louise showed by _____ it _____ that she wanted something to drink.

2. The woman was crying very hard, but she managed to <u>say through her sobs</u> that she needed help.

   The woman was crying very hard, but she managed to

   _____ that she needed help.

3. The tourists went into a little shop and bought some <u>things to give as gifts and things to remember the place</u>.

   The tourist went into a little shop and bought some _____ .

4. Visit the museum and <u>hunt through</u> the past.

   Visit the museum and _____ the past.

5. The man <u>looked</u> at the building <u>with unblinking eyes</u>.

   The man _____ at the building.

6. The largest <u>land mass</u> is Asia, and the smallest is Europe.

   The largest _____ is Asia, and the smallest is Europe.

7. He was filled with <u>a feeling of shock and surprise</u>.

   He was filled with _____ .

8. The sky was filled with a <u>sudden shower</u> of light.

   The sky was filled with a _____ of light.

9. The old building had two <u>toilets</u> on the first floor.

   The old building has two _____ on the first floor.

10. At the fancy restaurant, a man in a blue suit <u>says hello to</u> the guests.

    At the fancy restaurant, a man in a blue suit _____
    the guests.

11. I might never get another <u>opportunity</u> to visit Iceland.

    I might never get another _____ to visit Iceland.

12. The <u>wall hot water heater</u> works with gas and water pressure.

    The _____ works with gas and water pressure.

13. I didn't know what I was doing at the supermarket, but somehow I
    <u>was able</u> to buy everything I needed.

    I didn't know what I was doing at the supermarket, but somehow I

    _____ to buy everything I needed.

14. For a job interview, you want to <u>give</u> the people <u>a positive feeling
    about you</u>, so wear the right clothes and say the right things.

    For a job interview, you want to _____ the people, so
    wear the right clothes and say the right things.

Matching New Words and Meanings

A. Draw a line between the two words or phrases with similar meanings.

1. guffaw	a. shock; surprise
2. device	b. unfamiliar
3. the Balkans	c. acting out
4. souvenir	d. sudden display
5. disbelief	e. land mass
6. pantomime	f. tourist
7. burst	g. loud laugh
8. continent	h. countries of Southeastern Europe
9. traveler	i. simple machine
10. mystery	j. memento

B. Find the words and phrases in the two columns above that complete the sentences and write the correct form of each one in the blanks.

1. Both a _____ and a _____ are people who are not at home.

2. People keep both _____ and _____ to help them remember experiences.

3. _____ are the countries of Southeastern Europe.

4. When a person acts out drinking a glass without holding an actual glass in his hands, he is _____ .

5. A simple machine is a _____ .

6. Asia and Australia are _____ or _____ .

7. A joke can cause a _____ or a _____ .

8. Something that we have never seen before and do not understand is

   _____ to us, so we call such a thing a _____

   item.

9. A _____ or _____ of activity happens

   without warning.

10. Something that surprises a person causes _____ or

    _____ .

Finding the Differences

What's the difference between ...

1. a laugh and a guffaw?
2. a device and a machine?
3. a trip and a visit?
4. traveling and driving?
5. a country and a continent?
6. a restaurant and a dinner?

Matching New Words and Meanings

Draw a line between the two words or phrases with similar meanings.

1. flash heater   a. explore
2. travel   b. opportunity
3. mystery   c. divide
4. separate   d. unfamiliar
5. chance   e. device

Practicing with Idioms

Find the idiom in this list that completes each sentence and write the correct form of it in the blank. Note that some words (for example, [*something*]) can be replaced with other words and might be in another position in the sentence. You can use some of them more than once.

to burst into laughter	to brush up on
to buy souvenirs	to stare in disbelief
to choke [*something*] out	to talk baby talk
to act [*something*] out	to plan every detail
to show us into a room	

1. There are some television shows in which people try to

   _____ the name of a song or a movie.

2. If you _____ to a young child, the child will have a harder time learning to speak well.

3. One of the enjoyable parts of being a tourist is shopping in the little

   shops _____ to take home for family and friends.

4. I need _____ my French because I am going on a trip to Paris this year.

5. For the class trip, the students had _____ so that they could do all that they wanted to do in the time available.

6. At the museum, the guide _____ of extremely valuable old books.

7. The people in the kitchen _____ at my funny Polish sentences.

8. No one expected the woman to be able to speak Turkish. They heard

   her words, but they _____ at her _____ .

9. Before I try to teach you how to drive, I'd better _____ the rules myself.

10. I was so full of emotion that I could not even _____ my own name.

Exploring the Ideas

Think about these questions. Talk about your opinions with your classmates.

1. With a map of Europe, figure out the places that the four young travelers went. They started out from Istanbul and ended up in Zurich.

2. A flash heater is a work-saving device. Without a flash heater, heating water for a bath would be a big job. What are some other work-saving devices?

3. What are some things about a different country that will be unfamiliar to you?

4. What impresses you most about a new person?

Drawing Conclusions from the Story

Which of these statements are probably true, from the information in the story? Write *true* or *false* in the blank in front of each sentence.

1. _____ Jean probably really knew how to speak Polish.

2. _____ Louise, Stephanie, and Susan were students of language.

3. _____ All four of the young women were teachers.

4. _____ Jean's grandmother was a native speaker of English.

5. _____ Most train stations in Eastern Europe had tourism offices at that time.

6. _____ There weren't many tourist hotels in Eastern and Central Europe at that time.

7. _____ In Eastern and Central Europe, the water closet and bathroom were the same room.

8. _____ Polish and Turkish are probably not related languages.

9. _____ Jean's Polish sounded very funny to the people in Kraków.

10. _____ Jean was able to use her little bit of Polish well.

Taking a Close Look at the Meanings of the Words

1. The gas flames of the *flash heater* burn only when the water begins to flow. The word *flash* means "sudden light." The device gets its name from the *burst* of fire when the gas flames begin to burn.

2. Any *burst* is sudden: a *burst* of sunlight, a *burst* of flames, a *burst* of applause (when people suddenly begin to clap at a concert or sports event).

2. A person *greets* guests at the door. "Hello" and "Welcome" are common *greetings*.

3. The word *baby* as an adjective is used frequently in expressions like *baby teeth*, a *baby grand piano*, and *baby chair*. In some expressions, *baby* means small, as in a *baby* grand piano, which is smaller than a concert grand piano. Sometimes the word means that it is "of a baby," like *baby* teeth, the teeth that a baby gets before his or her adult teeth come in at about age seven.

A Good Cook

Preparing food is an art. Cooking is also a necessity. It can also be fun!

Before You Read the Story

Use these questions as preparation for reading the story. If you need to know the meaning of a word or idiom, check the Words and Idioms List after the story.

1. Which is this story likely to be about? First look at the title, go quickly through the pages of this section, and look at the pictures. Then make your choice.

   a. cooking or eating

   b. kinds of food or kinds of people

   c. learning or teaching

   d. a family or a school

   e. shopping or cleaning

2. What does a person need as tools (or utensils) to be a cook?

3. What supplies does every kitchen need to have? (These supplies are called "staples.")

While You Read the Story

Read these questions and look for the answers as you read the story.

1. Who is telling this story?

2. How did the storyteller become a good cook?

3. What did the storyteller's mother teach about cooking?

4. What makes a cook a can-opener cook?

A Good Cook

1   I don't know when I started to cook, but it was many many years ago. It might have been when my mother asked me to help her. She cooked everything from scratch. She baked bread and cakes and pies. And in our big family, the
5   oldest child often had to pitch in. So I probably started cooking before I was ten.

       Breakfast was never a formal meal at our house. My dad liked eggs, so he had eggs and coffee with several pieces of bread for breakfast. He was a working man, so he needed
10   that kind of food. The rest of us had toast with butter and jam and milk. I learned to make toast when I was five and to fry eggs over easy before I was ten, I'm sure.

       My mother asked me once to make a birthday cake for my sister's birthday. I had never baked anything before, so I
15   was nervous. But I followed a recipe exactly, and the cake was perfect.

       After that, I made a lot of cakes. Everyone especially liked the cinnamon cake with apples and sugar on top of it. I began to make that cake every
20   other day because a coffeecake like that never lasted more than two days at our house. I got so used to making that cake that I didn't even consult the recipe
25   book. Then one day, there were

no apples, so I started to make substitutions. One day I added dates, and another day I made a coffeecake with jam and nuts. I was becoming a cook because I was experimenting.

Then one day, my brothers asked if I would make pizza.

30 We lived far from cities where this new Italian food was common. We had never seen a pizza. At the store, I found a can of pizza sauce with a recipe on the label. It also had a tiny picture. I bought all the ingredients: tomato sauce, spices, olive oil, mozzarella cheese, and Italian sausage. We had

35 many of the staples, such as flour, yeast, and salt already at home in the pantry. First I made the dough. I had made bread with my mother, so pizza dough was easy. But since I had never seen a pizza (and the picture on the can was so small), I did a lot of experimenting. Of course, we had no

40 round pizza pans, but I used the big cake pans. And the boys loved the pizza! I was surprised myself by how good it was. Jim still says that the first pizza he ever tasted, the one I made, was the best he ever had.

My mother, with a family of eight, was glad to share her

45 kitchen with me. I learned to peel vegetables, to sear meat

roasts before putting them into the oven, and to use the pressure cooker. She taught me how to make cottage cheese (home cheese), and I learned

50 to make cheesecake. She showed me her recipe books, and I tried all kinds of foods. I think I decided to become a chemist because I loved to mix things together. The best part, of course, was the smiles on the faces of the family when something turned out really well.

55 After I left home, I got a few jobs working in restaurant kitchens. I was salad cook, then second cook, and then the ruler of the kitchen. I had become a chef. I loved to make mayonnaise and rich buttery French sauces. I had the time to cook then. It was my job.

60   Years later, I sometimes found myself without time to shop for food. And I certainly didn't have time to make elaborate meals. Oh, once in a while I would make a special dish— perhaps moussaka, a stuffed turkey, pizza, spaghetti, or meatballs. However, there were many days when cooking
65   from scratch just wasn't possible.

That's when I became a can-opener cook. I seldom open a can of stew, heat it, and serve it to my family. What I do is go into my pantry. I use canned foods and a can opener to assemble "homemade" recipes. I make chili in half an hour.
70   I use canned tomatoes, canned kidney beans, canned diced chilies, and a can of cooked chicken. I make five-bean salad out of five kinds of canned beans, canned beets, canned olives, and vinegar and oil (which come in bottles). Several years ago I began to collect recipes for those foods. Soon I began
75   joking about being a can-opener cook.

I am still writing my cookbook, but I share a lot of recipes with friends. Here are three of my favorite soup recipes for you. By the way, these recipes for soup can be recipes for stews or casseroles. Just reduce the amount of water and the number
80   of bouillon cubes (too much salt)! And add more vegetables.

Sauerkraut Soup

Drain and wash 1 can of sauerkraut (to get the salt out of it—I let it sit in fresh water for an hour while I clean up the kitchen. Then I run more cold water through it in
85   the colander.)

Boil one package of bratwursts or another type of sausage until the sausages look gray and cooked (there will be lots of fat that boils out of them). When they are cool, remove them from the pan, discard the water, and
90   slice the sausages into thin slices.

Put the boiled sliced bratwursts into a soup pot with 6 cups of water.

Add:

1 can of sliced mushroom pieces and stems with
95   the liquid

1 can of sliced white potatoes with the liquid
(or two cans if you want)

8 chicken or vegetable bouillon cubes

1 heaping tablespoon of onion powder

100   DO NOT ADD SALT until you have let it boil and get heated through and have tasted it. Eat and enjoy. I recommend dark rye bread with it...

Oriental Soup

1 cup of cut-up meat (beef, chicken, or pork)
105   6 cups of water

1/2 cup of cabbage sliced thin (or 1 can of
well-soaked and drained sauerkraut)

1 heaping T (tablespoon) of onion powder

10 bouillon cubes

110   1 can of Chinese vegetables

1 can of mushroom pieces and stems

First boil the meat in all the ingredients except the vegetables to cook it. Add the vegetables. Serve.

Mexican Chowder

115   6 cups of water

1 T onion powder

8 oz (or more) of raw sliced or cubed meat

1 can of white hominy with liquid

1 jar of chunky salsa

120   1 can of sliced white potatoes with liquid

10 bouillon cubes

Boil the meat in all the ingredients just long enough to cook the meat.

It's simple, it's fast, and it's delicious! What are your favorite recipes?

125

Words and Idioms List

You already know some of these words and idioms. Go through the list. Write a check (✓) next to each of those that you do not know.

Some of these words and idioms may be completely new for you. Find them in the reading. Use the sentences around them to understand what they mean. Note how they are used. These are the words and idioms to learn for this story.

1. _____ to **assemble** (verb): to collect pieces and put them together

2. _____ to **boil** (verb): to heat until bubbles of hot air form and continue to cook at that temperature

3. _____ a **bouillon cube** (noun): a small square of dried meat or vegetable juices with salt

4. _____ **bratwurst** (noun): a spicy sausage

5. _____ a **can opener** (noun): a device for opening canned foods

6. _____ a **casserole** (noun): a covered dish in which several foods, such as meat and vegetables, are baked together

7. _____ a **cheesecake** (noun): a dessert made of cheese, eggs, milk, flour, salt, sugar, and baking powder

8. _____ a **chef** (noun): a person who cooks professionally

9. _____ **chowder** (non-count noun): a thick soup

10. _____ **chunky** (adjective): not smooth; said of something that has large pieces

11. _____ a **coffeecake** (noun): a cake made in a flat pan, usually without any frosting or icing

12. _____ to **consult** (verb): to check with an authority; to ask for an opinion

13. _____ **cottage cheese** (noun): a white, plain cheese made of boiled milk

14. _____ a **date** (noun): a sweet fruit of one kind of palm tree

15. _____ **diced** (adjective): cut into tiny pieces or cubes

16. _____ to **discard** (verb): to throw away

17. _____ **dough** (non-count noun): unbaked bread

18. _____ to **drain** (verb): to separate something from liquid and throw away the liquid

19. _____ **eggs over easy** (idiom): eggs cooked in a frying pan with oil so that the whites and yolks stay separate but are cooked on both sides

20. _____ **elaborate** (adjective): fancy

21. _____ **hominy** (non-count noun): dried corn kernels that are boiled to become filled with water again

22. _____ an **ingredient** (noun): one item or part of a recipe

23. _____ to **make something from scratch** (idiom): to start with all the ingredients (not prepared foods)

24. _____ **moussaka** (non-count-noun): a Turkish or Greek dish made with eggplant

25. _____ a **mushroom** (noun): a fungus that can be eaten

26. _____ to **pitch in** (idiom): to help; to share work

27. _____ a **pressure cooker** (noun): a heavy pot that has a cover and that uses steam to cook food fast

28. _____ a **recipe** (noun): a plan for making a special kind of food

29. _____ **salsa** (noun): a sauce of tomatoes, peppers, onions, and spices used in Mexican cooking

30. _____ **sauerkraut** (non-count noun): salted and pickled cabbage

31. _____ a **sausage** (noun): a roll of preserved or fresh ground meat

32. _____ to **sear meat** (idiom): to put a piece of meat in a hot pan so that all parts of the outside of the meat get brown (and the juices stay in); to seal with heat

33. _____ to **slice** (verb): to cut into thin pieces

34. _____ a **slice** (noun): a thin piece

35. _____ a **stew** (noun): a meal of meat and vegetables cooked together

36. _____ a **substitution** (noun): something used in place of the real thing

37. _____ **toast** (non-count noun): slices of bread that have been exposed to heat and have turned brown

After You Have Read the Story

Do you have the answers to the questions from "While You Read the Story"? Talk about the answers with your classmates.

Understanding Sequence

In the blank in front of each sentence, write 2–10 to show that you know the order of the story.

a. _____ My brothers asked me to try making pizza, and I did it!

b. _____ My mother asked me to help her in the kitchen.

c. _____ I helped by peeling vegetables for my mother to use in cooking.

d. _____ My mother asked me to make my sister's birthday cake.

e. _____ I learned to fry eggs for my father's breakfast.

f. _____ Cooking for my family became difficult, so I became a
can-opener cook.

g. _____ I began making coffeecake every other day.

h. _____ I began experimenting and making substitutions.

u. __1__ I learned to make toast for breakfast when I was five.

j. _____ I got a job working in a restaurant.

Answering Questions About the Story

Read these questions, think about the answers, and then discuss the answers
with your classmates.

1. What are you likely to find in a pantry?
2. Find the names of five vegetables in the story.
3. Find the names of three kinds of desserts.
4. What kitchen tools or utensils can you find in the story?
5. There are several words for ways to cook.

   What do you do with a pot of water?

   What do you fry?

   What is roasted?

   What do you have to sear before you put it in the oven?

   What is making a cake called?
6. You can cook "on top of the stove" or "in the oven." What things are
   usually cooked on top of the stove? Which are usually cooked in an
   oven?
7. What word means removing the outside part of vegetables to prepare
   them to be cooked?
8. What are the usual ingredients for a cake?

Drawing Conclusions from the Story

Which of these statements are probably true, from the information in the story? Write *true* or *false* in the blank in front of each sentence.

1. _____ The storyteller did not want to learn to cook.

2. _____ There were six children in the family.

3. _____ A stew and a casserole have a lot in common.

4. _____ A colander probably has holes in it.

5. _____ If you cook something every day, you need a recipe for it.

6. _____ Bread and pizza are similar at the beginning.

7. _____ A pressure cooker can cook a meal fast.

8. _____ All coffeecakes have apples in them.

9. _____ You need beets for pizza.

10. _____ Cheese is a staple.

Finding the Meaning in Context

Find the word in the Words and Idioms List that means the same or almost the same as the underlined word or words and write it in the blank.

1. This recipe has onions as one of the <u>things that you need to make it</u>.

   This recipe has onions as one of the _____ .

2. This peanut butter is smooth, and that peanut butter is <u>not smooth because it has pieces of peanuts in it</u>.

   This peanut butter is smooth, and that peanut butter is

   _____ .

3. The device is a <u>tool for opening cans</u>.

   This device is a _____ .

4. How difficult is it to <u>collect in one place</u> the ingredients for making pizza?

   How difficult is it to _____ the ingredients for making pizza?

5. There is a lot of flour in <u>unbaked bread</u>.

   There is a lot of flour in _____ .

6. I don't know the meaning of that word, but I can <u>ask</u> my mother, the English teacher.

   I don't know the meaning of that word, but I can _____ my mother, the English teacher.

7. There is a type of <u>thick soup</u> made from clams.

   There is a type of _____ made from clams.

8. You can cook potatoes in ten minutes in a <u>heavy pot with a heavy cover that uses steam under pressure</u>.

   You can cook potatoes in ten minutes in a _____ .

9. Mexican food uses <u>a spicy sauce made of tomatoes, peppers, and onions</u> in many of its recipes.

   Mexican food uses _____ in many of its recipes.

10. The recipe called for white beans to put into the casserole, but I didn't have any. Kidney beans were the <u>beans that I used in place of white beans</u>.

    The recipe called for white beans to put into the casserole, but I didn't have any. Kidney beans were the _____ .

Matching New Words and Meanings

A. Draw a line between the two words with similar meanings.

1. soup		a. cube
2. roast		b. water
3. cabbage		c. cheesecake
4. corn		d. pot
5. dice		e. chowder
6. coffeecake		f. chef
7. cook		g. sauce
8. mayonnaise		h. bake
9. liquid		i. sauerkraut
10. pan		j. hominy

B. Find the words in the two columns above that complete the sentences and write the correct form of each one in the blanks.

1. Both a _____ and a _____ prepare food.

2. _____ is the vegetable, and _____ is the salted and preserved vegetable.

3. To _____ and to _____ both mean cooking in an oven.

4. You can drain both _____ and other _____ from boiled food.

5. Both _____ and a _____ add flavors to other foods.

6. _____ and _____ are two kinds of sweet foods.

7. A _____ and a _____ are two utensils
   for cooking.

8. One is a grain (_____) and the other is dried and
   then cooked (_____).

9. _____ is a food with lots of vegetables and liquid;
   _____ is a thick variety of the same kind of food.

10. To _____ and to _____ both mean to
    cut a large piece into smaller pieces.

Practicing with Idioms

Find the idiom in this list that means the same or almost the same as the
underlined words and use the correct form of it to complete each sentence.
Note that some words (for example, [*something*]) can be replaced with other
words and might be in another position in the sentence.

to run water through [something]	to pitch in
with [something] on the label	to joke about
to make [something] from scratch	to work in a kitchen
to let [something] sit	to follow a recipe
to come in cans or bottles	to turn out well

1. My grandmother found a recipe in a magazine and tried it. It <u>was
   successful</u>.

   My grandmother found a recipe in a magazine and tried it.

   It _____ .

2. The failure of my first casserole was a catastrophe at the time, but now
   I can <u>laugh about</u> it.

   The failure of my first casserole was a catastrophe at the time, but
   now I can _____ it.

3. Some preserved food, such as sauerkraut, is very salty, so I <u>put it in a colander and put it under the running faucet</u>.

   Some preserved food, such as sauerkraut, is very salty, so I

   _____ .

4. A good cook will tell you that after you roast a turkey, you should <u>not touch it or try to slice it</u> for about half an hour.

   A good cook will tell you that after you roast a turkey, you should

   _____ for about half an hour.

5. Most good cooks learn to cook at home, but some go to schools before they start to <u>cook professionally</u>.

   Most good cooks learn to cook at home, but some go to schools before

   they start to _____ .

6. At a supermarket you can find a great variety of foods that <u>are preserved and ready to be taken home for use</u>.

   At a supermarket you can find a great variety of foods that

   _____ .

7. I found a can of tomato sauce <u>that included</u> a recipe for pizza <u>on the outside</u>.

   I found a can of tomato sauce _____ a recipe for

   pizza _____ .

8. Cooking is easy; you just have to <u>do what the directions say</u>.

   Cooking is easy; you just have to _____ .

9. My mother asked me to make a cake <u>from flour, sugar, butter, eggs, baking powder, and cinnamon</u>.

   My mother asked me to make a cake _____ .

10. We can get this place cleaned up quickly if everyone <u>helps</u>.

We can get this place cleaned up quickly if everyone

_____ .

Exploring the Ideas

Think about these questions. Talk about your opinions with your classmates.

1. How is being a cook like being a chemist?
2. Why would a mother ask a child of ten to pitch in and help in the kitchen?
3. Why are some meals formal and other meals not?
4. Is it possible to follow a recipe and still not have the food turn out well? (How?)
5. Why does a good cook usually have staples and a full pantry at all times?
6. Which do you think is easier: to learn by watching another person prepare something or to learn by reading about it?
7. Is it safe for a child of five to make toast? (Under what conditions?)
8. What foods come in bottles or jars more often that in cans?
9. What do people usually think of as a can-opener cook?
10. If water can run through a colander, what do we know about colanders?

Making Inferences

Read the numbered sentence. Then read the sentences under it. Which ones are true because the numbered sentence is true? Circle the letter in front of each true statement.

1. I worked as a second cook.
   a. I had to make some foods two times.
   b. There were two cooks, and I was not the main cook.
   c. I was still learning some things about professional cooking.
   d. Two or more cooks worked together.

2. My mother made everything from scratch.

   a. She never used cake mixes.

   b. She used staples from the pantry to prepare the meals.

   c. She spent a lot of time cooking.

   d. She has time to make meals.

   e. She enjoyed reading recipes in cookbooks.

3. After I left home, my first job in a kitchen was as a salad cook.

   a. It is easy to make salads.

   b. Making salads takes a lot of training.

   c. I worked in a restaurant after I left home.

   d. Salad cooks work in kitchens.

   e. One cannot make salads at home.

4. A can-opener cook can't stuff a turkey.

   a. To prepare a stuffed turkey, you have to use canned foods.

   b. A turkey comes out of a can.

   c. There is some special work in stuffing a turkey and roasting it.

5. Boil a package of bratwursts until the sausages look gray and cooked so that the fat boils out of them.

   a. Bratwursts have a lot of fat in them.

   b. Cooked bratwurst should not be gray.

   c. People don't usually boil bratwursts.

   d. Bratwursts are sausages.

   e. You can buy sausages in packages.

Finding the Main Ideas

Write *MI* on the blank in front of each main idea, *SI* on the blank in front of each supporting idea, and *D* on the blank in front of each detail.

1. _____ I learned to be a can-opener cook because I didn't have much time to cook from scratch.

2. _____ The best part of cooking is the smiles on the faces of the eaters.

3. _____ I started cooking by making toast when I was five.

4. _____ My mother taught me a lot about cooking.

5. _____ I made pizza from a recipe and a picture.

6. _____ I have become a good cook because of many experiences.

7. _____ I made a birthday cake for my sister.

8. _____ My mother needed help in the kitchen, so I pitched in.

9. _____ I substituted dates for apples in the coffeecake that I made.

10. _____ Vinegar and oil come in bottles.

Reading for Details

Find the answers to these questions in the story.

1. How much water does each soup recipe require?
2. What did the storyteller use instead of pizza pans?
3. What kind of cheese is on pizza?
4. What did the storyteller substitute for apples in the coffeecake?
5. What does one make toast from?
6. What are some staples?
7. What can take the salt out of sauerkraut?
8. What is in five-bean salad?
9. What kind of bouillon cubes does the storyteller use?
10. What is a *heaping T* of onion powder?

Finding the Differences

What's the difference between...

1. baking and roasting?
2. onions and onion powder?
3. a casserole and a stew?
4. cabbage and sauerkraut?

5. a pot and a pressure cooker?

6. a coffeecake and a birthday cake?

7. a cook and a chef?

8. slicing and dicing?

9. soup and stew?

10. smooth and chunky?

Taking a Close Look at the Meaning of the Words

1. Some words in English are both nouns and verbs.

   A *drain* is a pipe that carries water away from a sink or washing machine. *To drain* is to allow water to escape from something that has water in it. Therefore, *drained* vegetables are canned vegetables with the liquid discarded (thrown away).

   A person goes to a *shop* (or supermarket, bakery, or grocery store) to shop for food. *To shop* means to go out for the purpose of buying.

   A *slice* of bread (or meat or a vegetable) is a thin section, cut off from the whole with a knife. The action that results in a *slice* is *slicing* (*to slice*). Do you like a slice of tomato on a hamburger? Do you like a slice of toast with your eggs?

   To cube is to cut into chunks. A brick of cheese can be sliced, or it can be cut lengthwise and crosswise to make *cubes*.

   To dice is to cut into tiny pieces, which may or may not be cubes. Usually cubes are larger. (By the way, the plural noun *dice* means something completely different!)

2. English has different words for the meat of some animals and the animal itself.

   > *Beef* is the meat of a cow.
   > *Mutton* is the meat of a sheep.
   > *Veal* comes from a young cow, a calf.
   > *Pork* is the fresh meat of a pig.
   > *Ham* is the smoked or preserved meat of a pig.

   However,

   > *turkey* comes from turkeys,
   > *chicken* comes from chickens, and
   > *lamb* comes from lambs, which are young sheep.

3. The expression *every other* means "alternating." For example, if you swim every other day and you swim on Mondays, you do not swim on Tuesdays or Thursdays. But you do swim on Wednesdays and Fridays.

4. Recipes use a lot of abbreviations. Sometimes *a cup* is just the letter *C*. A *teaspoon* is a small *t*, and a *tablespoon* is a capital *T*. Look at a recipe book for more abbreviations.

5. Mexican cooking uses a lot of peppers and other spices. *Chilies* are one kind of hot pepper. However, there is a soup or sauce (to put on rice) that is called *chili*. The peppers are a count noun: there are hot *chilies* in this salsa. The soup or sauce is a non-count noun: Would you like a bowl of *chili*?

"To Ja"

Perhaps this picture looks like any old family photograph, but it holds the story of finding a long-lost family member.

Before You Read the Story

Use these questions as preparation for reading the story. If you need to know the meaning of a word or idiom, check the Words and Idioms List after the story.

1. The words *To Ja* are pronounced "toe-yah." They are words in a foreign language. What can you guess from the fact that the story has two foreign words as the title?

2. Look at the pictures. What do the pictures tell you?

3. Read the first line of the story. Now what do you know?

While You Read the Story

Read these questions and look for the answers as you read the story.

1. Where does this story take place?

2. Who is the storyteller?

3. What is the storyteller searching for?

4. What does the storyteller find?

5. What do the words *to ja* mean? Why are they important to the story? Why doesn't the storyteller tell us the meaning at the beginning of the story?

"To Ja"

1   We were moving to Poland for two and a half years. I was going to work for the Peace Corps. My husband, two teenaged children, and I would be living in Warsaw. What excitement we all felt! For me, it was an opportunity to go to the country

5   of my forefathers. For the first time I felt the thrill of finding my own roots. How sad I felt that my father was gone. He had been dead for ten years already. It was hard to believe that it was that long because I still missed him a lot. He would have been happy to know we were going to

10   Poland. He had never been there himself, but his mother had always talked about the old country. I remembered many of her stories from her childhood. She had talked about the little farm and the lake.

15   I knew there would be opportunity to find relatives, however. I wanted to know what I could about the families of my parents. Both of my parents' families had come from Poland. I actually knew very

20   little. In fact, I knew nothing at all about my mother's side of the family except that her father had been born in a part of Poland that was in Austria. I knew that my maternal grandfather and his brother had come to the United States as young boys. My mother's mother's parents had come to the

25   United States around 1890. All official immigration records from that time were lost in a fire at Ellis Island. So there was no evidence on my maternal side. I had no clues as to where to find members of her family.

I had a few clues about the paternal side of the family. My father's father came from the village of Zukowo near the Baltic seaport city of Gdansk. I remembered stories about my paternal great-grandmother. She had been killed in a riot in

front of the Church of Saint Ann in Warsaw, the capital of Poland. I knew that the uprising happened around the turn of the century. I needed to know more, so I picked up the telephone.

I called my aunts, uncles, and cousins and asked for information. One cousin sent me the last letter that Grandma (my father's mother Josephine) had received from her sister Frances. The postmark was 1952—more than forty years ago! Another sent me a photograph of a family. The photograph was taken against the wall of a cottage. There were several people, young and old, in the picture. I took these with me to Poland.

Once we were settled in Warsaw and totally involved in learning the Polish language, I began my family search. I took the letter to an English-speaking priest, who translated it. He also wrote to the pastor of the church of the village the letter had come from. He asked about the cemetery in the village. He asked who was taking care of the grave of the woman who wrote the letter. The answer came back. The name of the man was Waclaw Dobrowulski. (His name is pronounced VATS-wahf DO-bro-VOOL-ski.) Waclaw was my father's first cousin, his mother's sister's son. And I now knew that he lived near the town of Sucha Rzecha. (It is pronounced SOO-ka ZSEK-ka and means "Dry River.")

60   Part of my job was visiting schools that had Peace Corps Volunteer teachers. So I did a lot of traveling. Several months after learning about my cousin Waclaw, I was in the northwest corner of Poland. I was near the border of Poland with Russia, Lithuania, and Belorussia. I had a free afternoon, and

65   I was near the city of Augustow. It was my chance to look for family. Dry River was near Augustow, so I went there. At the little post office, I asked where the Dobrowulski family lived. The woman at the post office told me to go six kilometers down the road to the next village. It was named Serwy

70   (SER-vee). The Dobrowulskis lived in Number 10.

The forest was cool and green as I drove to Serwy, wondering what I would find. When I got there, it seemed I would find no one. None of the dozen houses had numbers on them, and

75   no one was out and about. I drove around the village several times, seeing the pretty lake and the beautiful trees and gardens. Then I spotted someone in the backyard of a house on the edge of the lake. I stopped the car, got out, and went to the gate in

80   the fence. The old man came to the gate.

"Dzien dobry, Panu," I greeted him. He looked at me and looked at the car.

He returned my greeting.

"I have a letter and a photograph, "I said. I opened my bag

85   and pulled them out.

The man took the photograph from me. He looked deep into my green Polish eyes. He looked at the photograph. His eyes grew cloudy. He pointed to the young man in the photograph and said, "To ja. That's me."

Words and Idioms List

You already know some of these words and idioms. Go through the list. Write a check (✓) next to each of those that you do not know.

Some of these words and idioms may be completely new for you. Find them in the reading. Use the sentences around them to understand what they mean. Note how they are used. These are the words and idioms to learn for this story.

1. _____ a **capital** (noun): a city where a government is

2. _____ a **cemetery** (noun): the place where dead people are buried

3. _____ **cloudy** (adjective): unclear; filled with tears

4. _____ a **clue** (noun): information that helps to solve a problem or puzzle

5. _____ a **cottage** (n): a small country house

6. _____ **Ellis Island** (noun): an island in the harbor of New York (Many people who moved to the United States entered through Ellis Island for passport checking.)

7. _____ **evidence** (non-count noun): information to help solve a puzzle; clues

8. _____ **forefathers** (plural noun): ancestors; grandparents, great-grandparents, and so on

9. _____ a **free afternoon** (idiom): the time after noon without any business to do

10. _____ a **grave** (noun): a place where a person's body is put after death

11. _____ a **greeting** (noun): a hello or similar saying when meeting a person

12. _____ **immigration** (non-count noun): the act of moving into a new country to stay

13. _____ **maternal** (adjective): motherly; of the mother's family

14. _____ to **miss someone** (idiom): to feel the loss of someone; to want to be with a person and not be able to

15. _____ **official** (adjective): governmental; formal

16. _____ **the old country** (idiom): the country from which a person came

17. _____ a **pastor** (noun): a priest or minister who leads a church community

18. _____ **paternal** (adjective): fatherly; of or from the father's family

19. _____ a **postmark** (noun): a stamp of ink made at the post office that tells when a letter was sent and from where

20. _____ a **riot** (noun): a rebellion of the people against the government; a disturbance of order

21. _____ **roots** (plural noun): heritage; family history; ancestral home

22. _____ a **search** (noun): a hunt; the effort of trying to find something that is lost

23. _____ to **settle into a place** (idiom): to make a home in a new place

24. _____ a **side of the family** (idiom): either the mother's or father's family

25. _____ to **spot someone** (idiom): to see someone through distance or through a screen of some kind

26. _____ a **town** (noun): a small community, not big enough to be a city

27. _____ an **uprising** (noun): a rebellion; a riot; an act against the government

28. _____ a **village** (noun): a tiny community; a group of farmers' houses together in one place

After You Have Read the Story

Do you have the answers to the questions from "While You Read the Story"? Talk about the answers with your classmates.

Understanding Sequence

In the blank in front of each sentence, write 2–6 to show that you know the order of the story.

a. _____ They found out that the storyteller's paternal grandmother was from Sucha Rzecha.

b. _____ The storyteller's family settled in Warsaw and started to learn Polish.

c. _____ The storyteller had an opportunity to go to Sucha Rzecha.

d. _____ The storyteller asked relatives about family members who were still in Poland.

e. __1__ The storyteller got a job with the Peace Corps in Poland.

f. _____ The storyteller found Waclaw Dobrowulski, a cousin.

Finding Things in Common

What do these things have in common?

1. Augustow, Sucha Rzecha, and Serwy
2. mothers, grandmothers, and great-grandmothers
3. priests and pastors
4. Austria, Belorussia, and Lithuania
5. villages, towns, and cities
6. riots, uprisings, and rebellions
7. aunts, uncles, and cousins
8. a cottage, an apartment, and a house
9. information and evidence
10. uncles, sons, and brothers

Finding the Differences

What's the difference between ...

1. a garden and a yard?
2. an aunt and an uncle?
3. a city and a village?
4. maternal and paternal?
5. a father and a forefather?
6. a grave and a cemetery?
7. a family and a relative?
8. a cottage and a house?
9. an aunt and a sister?
10. a part of a country and a corner of that country?

Answering Questions About the Story

Read these questions, think about the answers, and then discuss the answers with your classmates.

1. Why was the photograph so important to the storyteller?
2. What did the photograph show?
3. What did the storyteller know about the maternal side of the family?
4. What happened in 1890 that was important to the storyteller's history?
5. What body of water is north of Poland?
6. Why did the storyteller travel a lot?
7. How far is Serwy from Dry River?
8. What is the Dobrowulskis' address?
9. What had the storyteller's grandmother said about her home in the old country?
10. When did the storyteller's father die?

Drawing Conclusions from the Story

Which of these statements are probably true, from the information in the story? Write *true* or *false* in the blank in front of each sentence.

1. _____ The storyteller's maternal relatives are probably not Polish.

2. _____ The riot in Warsaw happened inside a church.

3. _____ The members of the family came to the United States through Ellis Island.

4. _____ There was a river near Serwy, but it didn't have much water in it.

5. _____ Frances did not know how to write.

6. _____ The storyteller was afraid to search for members of her family.

7. _____ Houses in Serwy had numbers on them for the post office.

8. _____ The post office people knew where everyone in the village lived.

9. _____ Frances married someone named Zukowski.

10. _____ Waclaw is a woman's name.

Finding the Meaning in Context

Which meaning is closest to the underlined word or words? Circle *a, b, c,* or *d*.

1. Five people lived in the <u>cottage</u>.
   - a. village
   - b. house
   - c. town
   - d. apartment

2. The village <u>cemetery</u> has the burial places of all their forefathers.
   - a. church
   - b. garden
   - c. park
   - d. graveyard

3. The woman greeted the man, and he returned the <u>greeting</u>.
   - a. clues
   - b. stories
   - c. words of hello
   - d. letter and photograph

4. There were no <u>governmental</u> records about the family.

    a. evidence   c. official

    b. capital   d. written

5. The wedding was very beautiful, and many people's eyes seemed <u>filled with tears</u>.

    a. clear   c. cloudy

    b. happy   d. formal

6. The storyteller had some <u>evidence</u> about her father's family but nothing about her mother's family.

    a. names   c. clues

    b. official   d. government records

7. The <u>post office mark</u> on the letter was not easy to read.

    a. post office   c. postmark

    b. stamp   d. stampmark

8. Where did they finally <u>make their home</u> in the new country?

    a. search   c. settle

    b. miss   d. immigration

Matching New Words and Meanings

A. Draw a line between the two words or phrases with similar meanings.

   1. thrill   a. priest

   2. opportunity   b. mother's

   3. riot   c. clues

   4. pastor   d. chance

   5. evidence   e. excitement

   6. maternal   f. great-grandparents

   7. forefathers   g. uprising

   8. postmark   h. information

   9. relative   i. letter date

 10. records   j. cousin

B. Find the words and phrases in the two columns on page 203 that complete
the sentences and write the correct form of each one in the blanks.

1. In the _____ on Ellis Island, there is _____

    about many of the people who left the old country and came to the

    United States.

2. A _____ is a _____ , a member of one's

    family.

3. The _____ or _____ tells when a letter

    was sent.

4. Every church _____ is a _____ .

5. Two words that mean happy and positive feeling are

    _____ and _____ .

6. People can get hurt or even killed in a _____ or an

    _____ .

7. Relatives on one's _____ side of the family are

    _____ relatives.

8. A person's grandparents and _____ are his or her

    _____ .

9. The time to do something (when there is not much time or when

    the conditions are right) is either a _____ or an

    _____ .

10. To find a missing person, police need to have _____

    or some _____ .

Practicing with Idioms

Find the idiom in this list that means the same or almost the same as the underlined word or words and use the correct form of it to complete each sentence. Note that some words (for example, [*someone*]) can be replaced with other words and might be in another position in the sentence.

to grow cloudy	to have a free afternoon
to find [one's] roots	the turn of the century
to spot [someone]	to look deep into [someone's] eyes
to have no clues	to do a lot of [an action]
the old country	to settle into [a place]
to be gone	to be out and about

1. As a student, I have to <u>study a lot</u>.

   As a student, I have to _____ .

2. Would you like to go to a movie on Sunday, if you <u>don't have things that you have to do</u> then?

   Would you like to go to a movie on Sunday, if you _____ then?

3. My father died ten years ago, but it doesn't seem that he <u>has been dead</u> that long.

   My father died ten years ago, but it doesn't seem that he

   _____ that long.

4. The newly married couple went to Warsaw and <u>made their home in</u> a new part of town.

   The newly married couple went to Warsaw and _____ a new part of town.

5. The expression on the child's face began to look sad, as if he would start to cry.

   The expression on the child's face began to _____ .

6. I want to buy an old frame for this photograph, but I <u>don't know about</u> where to look.

   I want to buy an old frame for this photograph, but I

   _____ where to look.

7. My grandmother had a few photographs from her home in <u>the country where she was born</u>.

   My grandmother had a few photographs from her home in

   _____ .

8. At first the man <u>looked for an explanation for the situation in my face and my expression</u>.

   At first the man _____ .

9. His family came to Canada <u>around 1900.</u>

   His family came to Canada _____ .

10. In the village I didn't see any people, but then I <u>saw a man</u> in the backyard of a small house.

    In the village I didn't see any people, but then I _____
    in the back yard of a small house.

11. No one knows where Grandma is. She is <u>doing her shopping or visiting friends</u>.

    No one knows where Grandma is. She is _____ .

12. Many people from North America go to other countries to <u>find information about their forefathers</u>.

    Many people from North America go to other countries to

    _____ .

Exploring the Ideas

Think about these questions. Talk about your opinions with your classmates.

1. Why are a person's "roots" important? Why do so many people look for evidence about where their families came from?

2. How did the priest find out information about the storyteller's family? (What did he ask the parish priest in the village in his letter?) What clue does this fact give us about Polish culture?

3. The storyteller had heard stories from her grandmother. So what was the purpose in calling relatives on the phone?

4. Why did someone save the 1952 letter?

5. What is the effect of the fire that destroyed records at Ellis Island?

Making Inferences

Read the numbered sentence. Then read the sentences under it. Which ones are true because the numbered sentence is true? Circle the letter in front of each true statement.

1. When the storyteller's grandmother (Josephine) left Poland as a young woman, she was leaving the old country forever.

    a. Josephine knew that she would never see her family in Poland again.

    b. Frances wanted her sister to stay in Serwy.

    c. Josephine did not want to leave Serwy.

    d. Life in Serwy was not easy.

    e. Josephine was looking for a new life.

2. The pastor of the village of Serwy knew who was taking care of Frances's grave.

    a. Leaders in churches keep records about the people.

    b. Graves of one's relatives are kept neat.

    c. In Polish culture, one's family is important to the people.

    d. Frances was not living anymore.

3. When the storyteller's family was settled in Warsaw, they began to study the Polish language.

    a. They didn't know much Polish when they went to Poland.

    b. The storyteller's family found a house in Augustow.

    c. The storyteller, her husband, and her children always spoke Polish to one another.

    d. The storyteller's family liked studying Polish.

    e. The storyteller's family didn't like living in Warsaw.

4. I drove around the village of Serwy several times, seeing the pretty lake and the beautiful trees and gardens.

    a. There were no roads to Serwy.

    b. There is a lake in Serwy.

    c. The people in Serwy grow their own food.

    d. It wasn't easy to find an address in the village.

5. The old man's eyes grew cloudy.

    a. The sun was very bright.

    b. It began to rain.

    c. The man was surprised to see the photograph.

    d. The old man was starting to cry.

    e. Something was wrong with the old man's eyes, and he needed a doctor.

Finding the Main Ideas

Here are some other titles for this story. Which ones are appropriate? Which ones are not? Why not?

1. Finding Family

2. Alive in Poland

3. A Long-Lost Cousin

4. Our Time in Poland

5. One Free Afternoon

6. The Letter and the Photograph

7. Missing My Father

8. From Augustow to Serwy

9. Ellis Island

10. Going Back to the Old Country

Reading for Details

Find the answers to these questions in the story.

1. Where is the village of Zukowo?

2. When did the last letter come from the storyteller's side of the family?

3. How is the letter "w" pronounced in Polish?

4. When did the storyteller's maternal grandparents come to the United States?

5. What is Ellis Island?

6. What happened in front of the Church of Saint Ann in Warsaw?

7. Who was born in Austria?

8. Who was Josephine?

9. Why is Sucha Rzecha important in the story?

10. Where do the Dobrowulskis live?

11. What does *Sucha Rzecha* mean?

12. Where is Gdansk?

13. How long did the family stay in Poland?

Taking a Close Look at the Meaning of the Words

1. There are many words for relatives. Mothers and fathers have brothers and sisters. They are *aunts* (sisters) and *uncles* (brothers). Those *aunts* and *uncles* get married, and their husbands and wives are also *uncles* and *aunts*, by marriage. The children of aunts and uncles are *cousins* (both boys and girls). *Grandparents* (*grandmother* and *grandfather*) are the parents of one's parents. *Great-grandparents* are the parents of one's grandparents. A *first cousin* is the son or daughter of one's parent's brother or sister. The mothers of the storyteller's father and Waclaw were sisters (Josephine and Frances).

2. North America has become home to people from every continent. In the second half of the 1800s and in the early 1900s, great numbers of people came from countries in Europe. The potato famine in Ireland was one reason. Many Irish people came to North America because there was no food in the old country. At the same time, many people left Scotland, for example, and moved to Canada. They found land with weather that was similar to Scotland's. They settled on an island called Newfoundland and also in an area that they named Nova Scotia (New Scotland). The political trouble in Central Europe was another reason. For many people, Canada and the United States were lands of opportunity. The North American countries needed people, and they were welcomed.

The Power of Psychology

The professor seems to be running the class. But is he really in charge?

Before You Read the Story

Use these questions as preparation for reading the story. If you need to know the meaning of a word or idiom, check the Words and Idioms List after the story.

1. Psychology is a new area of study. It deals with the mind and emotions. It is the science of human and animal behavior. It is a social science, like anthropology and sociology. How is psychology different from the "hard" sciences (such as physics and chemistry)?

2. A scientist follows these steps. First he observes. Then he collects information (data). Next he makes a hypothesis (an educated guess). The last step is to test it. Why do all scientists follow these steps?

3. Can one study people? Is it OK to test animals? What do you think?

While You Read the Story

Read these questions and look for the answers as you read the story.

1. What is the laboratory for this experiment?

2. What is the experimental animal?

3. Who made the hypothesis?

4. How was the hypothesis proved?

The Power of Psychology

1   It was the first day of my first college class. I was one of 200 freshmen in Psychology 101. We were in a large lecture hall, and the professor started talking. First our professor said that psychology is a science. Because it is a science, it has
5   a base of experimentation. Many ideas, he said, can be tested through human behavior. He emphasized the importance of the scientific method. We should observe (watch), form a theory, and test it.

     Then he began to talk about the power of psychology. He
10   told us about the concept of behavioral control among people He wanted us to be interested in psychology because he was. That's why he began to explain human behavior to us. He explained how people interact with one another. The power of the mind, he emphasized, is very great.

15   "We are susceptible to other people's opinions, " he said. "We react to others. We can affect others' behavior," he continued. "When you listen to a person with interest, you show interest. Your eyes grow slightly larger. You lean forward, toward the
20   person. When you lose interest, your eyes close a little. You might lean away from the speaker. In this way, you, as the listener, can actually control the speaker. Body language speaks loud. The speaker is vulnerable to other people's reactions. Furthermore,
25   we are usually not aware of these effects. It all works in the subconscious mind."

     The members of the class were fascinated. We all had questions on the tips of our tongues. However, there was a knock on the door. It was the secretary of the psych department

30 at the door of the lecture hall. "Your telephone call from overseas has just come in," she said. The professor excused himself. He promised to return in just a few minutes. He then hurried from the room. We students began to talk about this idea that he had introduced. What a hypothesis! Someone

35 asked whether we could test it. Everyone laughed at that. But then someone else suggested a way. So together, we decided to test his theory about the power of body language. We would act in an experimental way in class. We would find out whether he was right about control of others' actions. We

40 would test him. He would be the experimental animal.

This is what we decided to do. We would lean forward and open our eyes wider when the teacher was lecturing. We would all sit up straight and take notes with great energy while he lectured. However, we would change when the

45 teacher went to the chalkboard to write or draw something. We would lean back in our seats. Our eyes would close too, but just a little bit. If the teacher went near the computer to use a PowerPoint program, we would react. We would slouch in our seats. Our body language would show less interest.

50 No sooner had we made this group decision than the professor returned. He apologized briefly. He said that he had been expecting this particular overseas telephone call for two weeks. He was at the lectern and looking at his lecture notes. So we all leaned forward in interest. We opened our

55 eyes as wide as we could. He looked up at us, somewhat surprised. Then he began to tell us details about the phone call. He told us who it was from. He explained that the person was studying tribal people in the jungle. That was why it was so hard to get in touch with her. We kept our eyes wide open.

60   And he went on. Then he told us what the message was about. Our interest was obvious to him. He told us much more than he normally would have. He shared details of his personal conversation with this person overseas. Then he turned to the chalkboard. We all leaned back in our chairs.
65   We seemed disinterested. He went to the computer to show us pictures on the screen, and we slipped deeper into our seats. He seemed somewhat confused, but the bell rang. Class was over. He had been saved by the bell.

Throughout the whole semester, we continued responding
70   to his actions in class. We were careful not to react to his movements suddenly, but rather naturally. When the professor spoke to us, we showed great interest. We always leaned forward when he was at the lectern. We relaxed into our seats when he moved away from it. When he was at the
75   chalkboard or anywhere not at the lectern, we appeared to be less interested.

By the end of the semester, the professor was lecturing without stopping. He gripped the sides of the lectern. The knuckles on his hands were white. He seemed to be high
80   energy and almost nervous. He didn't use the chalkboard at all, and he no longer turned on the computer.

The class chose a spokesperson for the last day of class. Then, on that last day, we told the teacher that he had been right. Our spokesperson explained: We had not believed him
85   on the first day. We didn't believe that we students could control his behavior through our body language. However, his response to our actions had proved that he was right. He lectured and did not use any other instructional means.

90 For a moment, the professor was astonished. For a few seconds his face showed feelings of anger and shock. His brow furrowed, but then the lines disappeared. He laughed. As he left the room, he shook his head in disbelief. Psychology is based on observation and testing theories. We proved the theory.

Words and Idioms List

You already know some of these words and idioms. Go through the list. Write a check (✓) next to each of those that you do not know.

Some of these words and idioms may be completely new for you. Find them in the reading. Use the sentences around them to understand what they mean. Note how they are used. These are the words and idioms to learn for this story.

1. _____ to **affect** (verb): to cause; to influence

2. _____ to **apologize** (verb): to say one is sorry

3. _____ a **base** (noun): a foundation; a beginning

4. _____ to **be aware** (idiom): to know about

5. _____ a **brow** (noun): the top part of a person's face, between the hair and the eyes

6. _____ a **concept** (noun): an idea

7. _____ **confused** (adjective): not sure or not knowing what is happening

8. _____ **disinterested** (adjective): not interested

9. _____ an **effect** (noun): a result

10. _____ to **emphasize** (verb): to give importance to

11. _____ to **excuse oneself** (verb): to ask permission to leave, or to say one is sorry

12. _____ **experimentation** (non-count noun): trying different things

13. _____ a **freshman** (noun): a first-year student

14. _____ to **furrow** (verb): to make lines in the soil (or make lines in one's forehead skin)

15. _____ to **grip** (verb): to hold onto tightly

16. _____ to **interact** (verb): to talk with

17. _____ a **jungle** (noun): a forest near the equator

18. _____ a **knuckle** (noun): a finger joint

19. _____ to **lean** (verb): to bend one's body

20. _____ a **lectern** (noun): a tall table with a slanted top for a teacher to stand at

21. _____ a **lecture** (noun): a formal lesson given to a large class

22. _____ to **observe** (verb): to watch carefully for evidence

23. _____ **on the tip of one's tongue** (idiom): said about a name or idea that one cannot quite remember

24. _____ to **react** (verb): to answer; to act after another person

25. _____ a **reaction** (noun): a response

26. _____ **saved by the bell** (idiom): said when a time limit means that something doesn't have to be done because the time has ended

27. _____ **science** (non-count noun): formal study of life and the universe

28. _____ to **slouch** (verb): to sit with one's back bent and feet out in front

29. _____ a **spokesperson** (noun): a person chosen to speak for a group

30. _____ a **subconscious mind** (noun): the part of the mind that the person is not aware of

31. _____ **susceptible** (adjective): able to be influenced

32. _____ a **theory** (noun): an idea without full proof of its truth; an educated guess

33. _____ **vulnerable** (adjective): likely to be hurt; in danger

After You Have Read the Story

Do you have the answers to the questions from "While You Read the Story"? Talk about the answers with your classmates.

Understanding Sequence

In the blank in front of each sentence, write 2–10 to show that you know the order of the story.

a. _____ The students made up some rules for the whole class to follow to encourage lecturing from the front of the room.

b. __1__ The storyteller signed up for a beginning psychology class.

c. _____ On the first day, the professor explained about the influence of body language.

d. _____ The teacher was shocked at first, and then he left the room laughing.

e. _____ By the end of the semester, the teacher was only lecturing.

f. _____ The professor left the classroom to answer an overseas telephone call.

g. _____ While he was gone, the students decided to test the hypothesis about behavior control.

h. _____ The class was interested in behavior control through body language and wanted to ask questions.

i. _____ They followed these rules of behavior through the whole semester.

j. _____ A spokesperson for the class explained the experiment to the teacher.

k. _____ The professor responded to the behavior of the students.

Answering Questions About the Story

Read these questions, think about the answers, and then discuss the answers with your classmates.

1. What kind of response did the students have to the professor's hypothesis?
2. Were these good students?
3. Why did the professor leave the lecture?
4. Do professors usually leave their lectures? What was unusual about this situation?
5. How do we know that the students had understood the lecture up to that point?
6. Why did the students have to pay close attention to the professor?
7. How do we know that body language speaks to the subconscious mind?
8. What does the storyteller tell us about his reactions?
9. What is the storyteller's purpose in telling us about his psychology class?
10. Do you think the storyteller enjoyed his psychology class? Why or why not?

Drawing Conclusions from the Story

Which of these statements are probably true, from the information in the story? Write *true* or *false* in the blank in front of each sentence.

1. _____ Body language does send a message.

2. _____ The professor did not expect his students to test the theory on himself.

3. _____ Freshman students don't know what they are doing.

4. _____ The experiment probably continued all semester because the students could see that they were making a difference in the professor's behavior in class.

5. _____ The professor wanted the students to do experiments.

6. _____ The students thought it would be fun to do an experiment.

7. _____ No one wanted to be the spokesperson.

8. _____ The class showed that the professor was susceptible to his students' opinions.

9. _____ There are no ways to show interest or disinterest without words.

10. _____ Teachers do not lecture while they are at the chalkboard.

Finding the Meaning in Context

Which meaning is closest to the underlined word or words? Circle *a, b, c,* or *d.*

1. The instructor said to <u>take a firm hold of</u> the ladder before going down.
   - a. furrow
   - b. observe
   - c. emphasize
   - d. grip

2. The teacher <u>appeared</u> to be ready to start.
   - a. seemed
   - b. wanted
   - c. is willing
   - d. was not able

3. The teenager <u>said that he was sorry</u> for being noisy in school.
   - a. confused
   - b. interested
   - c. slouched
   - d. apologized

4. There are many animals in the <u>tropical forest</u>.
   - a. jungle
   - b. lecture
   - c. base
   - d. farm

5. The <u>response</u> of the audience was difficult to understand.
   - a. effect
   - b. reaction
   - c. science
   - d. experimentation

6. There was a bright red line across her <u>brow</u>.
   - a. forehead
   - b. elbow
   - c. face
   - d. arm

7. You <u>aren't sitting up straight</u>!

    a. 're reacting   c. 're gripping

    b. 're slouching   d. 're emphasizing

8. The teacher asked the class to <u>forgive him</u> for leaving for a few minutes.

    a. confuse him   c. excuse him

    b. interact with him   d. save him by the bell

9. They chose one <u>person to talk for all of them</u>.

    a. speaker   c. spokeman

    b. spokesperson   d. speakerperson

10. The professor <u>put his back</u> against the wall <u>and rested</u> as he taught the class.

    a. slouched   c. gripped

    b. leaned   d. affected

Matching New Words and Meanings

A. Draw a line between the two words or phrases with similar meanings.

1. vulnerable	a. idea
2. concept	b. observe
3. lean	c. respond
4. watch	d. susceptible
5. hypothesis	e. slouch
6. freshman	f. appear
7. slip down	g. bend
8. interested	h. theory
9. react	i. fascinated
10. seem	j. first-year student

B. Find the words and phrases in the two columns on page 221 that complete the sentences and write the correct form of each one in the blanks.

1. Both a _____ and a _____ are ideas that need to be proved.

2. A person who can easily be hurt is _____ or

   _____ .

3. A _____ and an _____ are the products of thinking.

4. Both _____ and _____ can be verbs for actions of people sitting in chairs.

5. In a college or university, a first-year student is a _____ .

6. Two words that mean a person wants to know more about a topic

   are _____ and _____ .

7. First one person says something, and then the other people

   _____ or _____ to her. (They do something as a result of the first person's words or actions.)

8. There are five children in the playroom. The psychologists are

   _____ them and _____ their behavior through a mirrored window.

9. In a dance class, the students learn how to _____ or

   _____ and still stay on balance.

10. If a road looks wet, it _____ or _____ to have water on it.

Practicing with Idioms

Find the idiom in this list that means the same or almost the same as the underlined word or words and use the correct form of it to complete each sentence. Note that some words (for example, [*someone*]) can be replaced with other words and might be in another position in the sentence.

> to be over
> to be aware of
> to show great interest
> to have white knuckles
> to get in touch with [someone]
> to shake [one's] head in disbelief
> to be saved by the bell
> to have [something] on the tip of [one's] tongue

1. I <u>wanted to ask</u> a question <u>but I couldn't think of a way to ask it</u>.

   I _____ a question _____ .

2. The professor was very surprised by the students and <u>moved his head from side to side because he couldn't believe what they had done</u>.

   The professor _____ his head _____ .

3. In class, I was asked a difficult question, but I <u>didn't have to answer it because the bell rang</u>.

   In class, I was asked a difficult question, but I _____ .

4. I went skiing, but I <u>was very frightened by it</u>.

   I went skiing, but I _____ .

5. When I visited Paris, I <u>tried to find</u> an old friend.

   When I visited Paris, I tried _____ an old friend.

6. In all places and at all times, some teachers <u>must pay attention to</u> children.

   In all places and at all times, some teachers _____ children.

7. The tourists <u>seemed to be very interested</u> in going on short trips around the island.

   The tourists _____ in going on short trips around the island.

8. The movie <u>was finished</u> by nine o'clock.

   The movie _____ by nine o'clock.

Exploring the Ideas

Think about these questions. Talk about your opinions with your classmates.

1. What do you think about the students' behavior? Was it polite?
2. Why do you think the professor's first response was shock and anger?
3. Why did the professor change his mind?
4. The students actually broke an important rule. In a psychology test, the human subject (the experimental animal) must agree to participate in the experiment. Did the professor agree? Why do you think such a rule is important? (Or is it?)
5. How is psychology an "indirect" science? Why must it be so?
6. Their experience on the first day of class encouraged the students to continue through the whole semester. What happened that first day to convince them to continue?
7. What was the hypothesis? How did the students form it?
8. Why couldn't the professor be upset with the students?
9. Do you think it is right to try to control others' behavior? Why or why not?
10. When do we NOT try to control the behavior of others?

Making Inferences

Read the numbered sentence. Then read the sentences under it. Which ones are true because the numbered sentence is true? Circle the letter in front of each true statement.

1. We all had questions on the tips of our tongues, but the class was interrupted.

    a. The students were biting their tongues.

    b. The students were glad that the secretary called the professor away.

    c. The students wanted to ask a lot of questions.

    d. The students were disinterested in the theory of body language.

    e. The students were fascinated by the concept of control through body language.

2. Body language speaks loud.

    a. Body language can hurt your ears.

    b. What a person "says" through actions is easily understood.

    c. There is a way to communicate without words.

    d. "Speaking" can happen without using one's mouth.

3. The teacher shared information and details of his personal telephone conversation with a person overseas.

    a. The teacher had called a person on the other side of the world.

    b. The teacher told the class about his conversation.

    c. The teacher went overseas to tell the person about his class.

    d. The class asked the teacher about his conversation on the telephone.

    e. The class showed that they were interested, so the teacher continued talking.

4. By the end of the semester, the professor was lecturing non-stop.

    a. The professor lectured from the beginning to the end of the class.

    b. The teacher lectured all day long.

    c. The professor loved to lecture.

    d. The professor's behavior in class changed over the semester.

5. The professor's first reaction was shock and anger, but then he laughed.

    a. The professor probably felt that the students had made a fool of him.

    b. The professor was always angry first.

    c. The professor understood that the students had really listened to his first lecture.

    d. The professor didn't understand what the students had done.

6. Body language works on the subconscious mind.

    a. A person is not always aware of body language.

    b. Most people do not react to body language.

    c. Many people respond without thinking to body language.

    d. There are many effects of body language.

Finding the Main Idea

Which of these titles are appropriate for this story? Write *too small, too big,* or *just right* for each title.

Title	Your judgment of the title
1. One Day in Class	1. _____
2. An Experiment by the Students	2. _____
3. Using PowerPoint in a Lecture	3. _____
4. How I Learned About Experimenting	4. _____
5. The Field of Psychology	5. _____
6. A Professor Learns a Lesson	6. _____
7. An Important Telephone Call	7. _____
8. The Power of Body Language	8. _____
9. What the Spokesperson Said	9. _____
10. My University Years	10. _____

Reading for Details

Find the answers to these questions in the story.

1. What was the name of the course the storyteller took?
2. When did he take this course?
3. What did the professor use the computer for in class?
4. How many students were there in his class?
5. Whose idea was the testing of the professor's hypothesis?
6. How did the students respond to the professor when he moved away from the lectern?
7. What was the cause of their slouching? What was the effect of their slouching?
8. What interrupted the class?
9. What was special about this phone call?
10. At the end of the semester, the professor's knuckles were white as he gripped the lectern. What do white knuckles show?

Taking a Close Look at the Meaning of the Words

1. *Psyche* is the name of a character in Roman mythology. She was a human girl, and her beauty got her into trouble with Venus. Venus, the Roman goddess of love and beauty, didn't like this girl. Venus wanted all men to love herself and not human women. Psyche fell in love with Cupid, who was the son of Venus. Venus, in her jealousy, made life miserable for Psyche. But Jupiter (the father of the Roman gods) rescued Psyche and made her immortal. The word *psyche* means the soul of a person. The science of psychology is an attempt to understand human emotions.

2. An *experiment* is a trial or a test. Experimental evidence is information (or data) from a test. For scientists to accept the data as evidence or proof, it must be collected according to specific rules. Anecdotes are stories. *Anecdotal evidence* comes from everyday experiences. Scientists do not accept evidence from stories because the conditions are not controlled.

3. Sometimes a person wants to remember a name, a place or an idea. However, the idea does not come out. It stays "on the tip of the person's tongue." The idea is just below awareness. Psychologists tell us that there is a way to "catch" the words on the tip of one's tongue. First raise your eyes as if looking up. Then roll them all the way around to the right ride, to the bottom, to the left side, and then to the top again. Usually, within a few minutes, the idea or words will come to your conscious mind.

The Story of Harvey the Pigeon

Pigeons are very good at telling the differences among colors. Therefore, they are good experimental animals. We can learn a lot about behavior from watching what animals do.

Before You Read the Story

Use these questions as preparation for reading the story. If you need to know the meaning of a word or idiom, check the Words and Idioms List after the story.

1. What does a green light mean to you?

2. What difference does it make to you if the light turns red?

3. Do you know anyone who cannot tell the difference between colors? (That person is colorblind.) How does colorblindness make problems for a person? Is it important to be able to tell the difference between colors?

4. What does the title of this story make you think about?

While You Read the Story

Read these questions and look for the answers as you read the story.

1. Who is Harvey?

2. Why is Harvey a matter of concern to the scientists?

3. Why are they watching Harvey so closely?

4. What do they learn about pigeons from Harvey?

5. Does there seem to be a lesson for people from this experiment? What is it?

6. Is there evidence that other pigeons are like Harvey?

The Story of Harvey the Pigeon

1   Three researchers were working in an animal research laboratory. They were animal psychologists. Their job was to study one group of animals. In the lab, they were studying how pigeons learn. These birds are good subjects. First of all,
5   they are very intelligent birds. Pigeons are especially good in discrimination. That is, they can tell the difference between two similar things. They can discriminate easily. They can distinguish colors, too. That is why they are good birds to study.

  The researchers had some facts about these birds. Hungry
10   birds easily learn to press a bar for food. So the scientists put a bar in the cage. Every time the bird's beak touched the bar, a grain of food dropped into the cage. Pigeon eyesight is keen. They would see the grain and eat it. They also see a wide range of colors. Because of their sharp discrimination skills,
15   they will act differently in different situations. They can detect small differences in the similar shapes of two things better than any other birds. Therefore, they can tell which thing is a ball and which is a bird.

  One of the pigeons knew how to peck for food. They
20   called this pigeon Harvey. A green light was on in Harvey's cage. Harvey seemed to be happy in the green light. Then the scientist changed the color of the light to red. And the bar pressing dropped no grain. After many times of not being fed when the light was red, Harvey learned to wait. When the
25   light turned green, he started pecking for more food. The pigeon, however, did not seem to wait patiently through a red light. While he waited for the signal light to turn green and for food to be available, Harvey walked around in circles. He walked back and forth.

25   In fact, that pigeon seemed to be agitated. That is, he paced back and forth, his head looking first in one direction and then another. The bird pecked at the wire of the cage. And he pecked at things like the floor of the cage while waiting. The pecking at the floor seemed to continue even after the

30 pigeon knew about the red lights. Harvey had waited many times for the red light to turn green. The bird waited, and eventually the light turned green. Then bar pressing brought food. One time, a naïve observer was there. This visitor did not understand how psychologists talk about animal behavior.

35 To the visitor, Harvey looked quite frustrated.

    The researchers set up a series of experiments. They wanted to study Harvey's range of behaviors. In one of these experiments, another pigeon was put into the cage with Harvey. This neutral, uneducated bird was restricted so that it

40 could not interfere with Harvey. The new pigeon was simply there. Harvey seemed to ignore the new pigeon. Everything in the two-pigeon cage went along fine as long as the green light was on and Harvey was getting food for pecking.

    However, as soon as the green light was switched off,

45 and the red light was turned on, Harvey took one look at the other bird and promptly killed it.

    Harvey's violent behavior shocked the researchers. They liked Harvey, but he was acting war-like. Was Harvey the only bird with such a response? They needed to know. Therefore,

50 they did more experiments with another pigeon. This time the new pigeon was restrained, but it was also protected. The test showed that the effect of the second pigeon in the cage was not an accident. They tried the experiment with other pigeons that knew to press a bar for food during a green

55 light. And the response for all these pigeons was the same.

They all behaved like Harvey. They were aggressive toward other pigeons when the red light went on. They acted the same way toward pigeon-shaped objects. The pigeons were not getting a reward that they expected.

60   Was the extra pigeon in the cage connected to the red light and the end of the feeding? It was clear to people that there was no connection. However, 65 to the birds there was a clear link between the red light and the stopping of food, and the red light and the extra bird. To the pigeons, the extra bird made the red light turn on and the food supply stop.

70   There is a moral to the story of the pigeons. In experiences with other people, especially with those who are close to us, we are likely to behave like Harvey. No matter where the sense of frustration comes from, we show it toward others. We seem to have a Harvey inside us. Something goes wrong, 75 and we feel like striking out at those who are near us. In fact, "pigeoning" is at the root of a lot of marriage and family troubles. It is human to want to blame someone else for a problem.

There is a lesson to learn from Harvey. As human beings who can learn, we can find ways of handling angry feelings. To make our families and other close friends feel safe with us, we find gentle ways of expressing ourselves.

Words and Idioms List

You already know some of these words and idioms. Go through the list. Write a check (✓) next to each of those that you do not know.

Some of these words and idioms may be completely new for you. Find them in the reading. Use the sentences around them to understand what they mean. Note how they are used. These are the words and idioms to learn for this story.

1. _____ **aggressive** (adjective): willing or ready to fight

2. _____ to **agitate** (verb): to cause trouble

3. _____ a **beak** (noun): the hard mouth of a bird

4. _____ to **connect** (verb): to link; to tie together

5. _____ a **connection** (noun): a link; a tie

6. _____ to **detect** (verb): to see some small bit of evidence

7. _____ **discrimination** (non-count noun): act of not treating all things equally; act of telling the difference

8. _____ **eventually** (adverb): not now, but later in time

9. _____ **eyesight** (non-count noun): ability to see

10. _____ **frustrated** (adjective): angry because of not being able to do what one wants

11. _____ **intelligent** (adjective): sharp in mind; having clear thinking

12. _____ to **interfere** (verb): to make something stop; to break in

13. _____ **keen** (adjective): sharp; intelligent

14. _____ a **laboratory** (noun): a place where scientists do experiments

15. _____ a **moral** (noun): a lesson

16. _____ **naïve** (adjective): simple; uneducated

17. _____ **neutral** (adjective): not positive and also not negative

18. _____ **patiently** (adverb): without any emotional response

19. _____ to **peck** (verb): to pick up pieces of food from the ground with a beak

20. _____ a **pigeon** (noun): a large, intelligent bird

21. _____ to **press** (verb): to push down on

22. _____ **promptly** (adverb): immediately; quickly

23. _____ a **researcher** (noun): a scientist who is doing an experimenting; testing

24. _____ **restrained** (adjective): tied down

25. _____ a **reward** (noun): a prize for doing something good

26. _____ a **subject** (noun): a person or animal that is being observed

27. _____ to **switch off** (verb): to stop the flow of

28. _____ **war-like** (adjective): fighting; violent

After You Have Read the Story

Do you have the answers to the questions from "While You Read the Story"? Talk about the answers with your classmates.

Understanding Sequence

In the blank in front of each sentence, write 2–11 to show that you know the order of the experiment.

a. _____ Harvey ignored the other pigeon when the light was green.

b. _____ The scientists came to some conclusions about pigeons and red lights.

c. __1__ The researchers set up the experiment.

d. _____ The scientists came to some conclusions about pigeons and red lights.

e. _____ The researchers put another pigeon into the cage, but this pigeon couldn't move around the cage.

f. _____ First they made a cage with a bar to press for food.

g. _____ Other pigeons who were trained like Harvey did the same thing.

h. _____ The scientists came to some conclusions about pigeons and red lights.

i. _____ They turned on a green light and rewarded Harvey with a grain of corn for each bar press.

j. _____ Harvey attacked the other pigeon when the light turned red.

k. _____ They didn't give Harvey any grain when the light was red.

l. _____ Harvey seemed agitated when the light was red.

Answering Questions About the Story

Read these questions, think about the answers, and then discuss the answers with your classmates.

1. What were the researchers studying?
2. What do the researchers know about pigeon's eyes?
3. In what way are pigeons smart?
4. What is the difference in shape between a ball and a bird?
5. What had to touch the bar for food to appear? Under what conditions did food appear?
6. Are birds and balls similar in shape?
7. What did Harvey do while he waiting for the light to change?
8. Why was the second bird restrained?
9. Why was the third bird protected and restrained?
10. How was Harvey like a frustrated and angry person?

Drawing Conclusions from the Story

Which of these statements is probably true, from the information in the story? Write *true* or *false* in the blank in front of each sentence.

1. _____ Harvey hated other pigeons.

2. _____ Harvey was like all other pigeons.

3. _____ The scientists tried to make Harvey angry.

4. _____ The change in the light made no difference to the pigeons.

5. _____ Harvey liked to have food to eat.

6. _____ Harvey couldn't discriminate between red and green.

7. _____ The other pigeons took Harvey's grain.

8. _____ Hungry birds are better learners.

9. _____ The cage was made of wire.

10. _____ Naïve observers might not understand the collection of data.

Finding the Meaning in Context

Which meaning is closest to the underlined word or words? Circle *a, b, c,* or *d.*

1. There is a <u>lesson</u> to this story.
   a. learning
   b. moral
   c. switch
   d. end

2. Harvey was <u>violent</u> when he was not rewarded for pressing the bar.
   a. frustrated
   b. patient
   c. war-like
   d. accidental

3. The researchers were <u>very surprised</u> by Harvey's behavior.
   a. shocked
   b. pleased
   c. agitated
   d. restrained

4. A pigeon's <u>ability to see clearly</u> is a reason for using pigeons in an experiment.
   a. discrimination
   b. reward
   c. eyesight
   d. promptness

5. The <u>person or animal who is being studied</u> is observed carefully.

   a. observer

   b. researcher

   c. scientist

   d. subject

6. A <u>person who is watching but doesn't know</u> is not able to judge well.

   a. naïve observer

   b. visitor

   c. professor

   d. researcher

7. The bird responded <u>promptly</u>.

   a. correctly

   b. simply

   c. quickly

   d. with violence

8. The pigeon can <u>discriminate</u> between two colors well.

   a. agitate

   b. separate

   c. detect

   d. tell the difference

9. Some people <u>act</u> like Harvey when they don't get what they want.

   a. are

   b. strike out

   c. agitate

   d. detect

10. The green light was <u>turned</u> off.

   a. connected

   b. detected

   c. switched

   d. pecked

Matching New Words and Meanings

A. Draw a line between the two words or phrases with similar meanings.

1. scientist	a. tell the difference
2. keen	b. bird
3. discriminate	c. researcher
4. angry	d. moral
5. lesson	e. get in the way
6. pigeon	f. restricted
7. naïve	g. war-like
8. violent	h. frustrated
9. interfere	i. uneducated
10. restrained	j. sharp

B. Find the words in the two columns on page 238 that complete the sentences and write the correct form of each one in the blanks.

1. If a person does something to stop another person's work, the first

   person _____ or _____ .

2. A person who strikes out at another person is _____

   and _____ .

3. The extra pigeon in the cage was tied down. That is, it was

   _____ or _____ .

4. A person who does not understand because she has not been taught

   is _____ or _____ .

5. Both _____ and _____ are words that

   express negative emotions.

6. A _____ is a kind of bird.

7. Both _____ and _____ do experiments

   in laboratories.

8. A person with intelligence and quick ability is _____

   or _____ .

9. Pigeons have the ability to tell the difference or _____

   between colors.

10. We can learn an important _____ from the story of

    Harvey. The _____ is that we blame others.

Figuring Out the Relationship

There are connections between things that follow these patterns:
    part to whole
    cause and effect
    boss and worker
    class of things and an example

There are many other relationships, too. Can you figure out what the relationship is between...

1. a bird and a beak?
2. a researcher and a laboratory?
3. a reward and a grain of corn for a pigeon?
4. a light and a switch?
5. pressing a bar and a reward of a grain of corn?
6. good discrimination skills and keen eyesight?
7. an experiment and a theory?
8. a subject and a scientist?
9. sharp and keen?
10. neutral and naïve?

Exploring the Ideas

Think about these questions. Talk about your opinions with your classmates.

1. Some people think that psychological experiments with people and animals are unethical. (They think it is wrong to do such experiments.) How do you feel about this topic?
2. Some animals can be taught well. Do you know anyone with a trained animal? What can the animal do?
3. What reason is there for researchers to study pigeons?
4. Do you know people who "pigeon" others—that is, blame other people for the bad things that happen to them? Harvey didn't understand that the extra pigeon was not turning on the red light. Harvey just knew that the bird was there and the red light stopped the food. To the bird, there was a connection. What did the bird "think," or did it think at all?
5. What did you learn from the story of Harvey the pigeon?

Making Inferences

Read the numbered sentence. Then read the sentences under it. Which ones are true because the numbered sentence is true? Circle the letter in front of each true statement.

1. Pigeons' eyesight is keen.

    a. Pigeons can see tiny grains on the sidewalk.

    b. Pigeons peck at tiny bits of food.

    c. Pigeons don't eat food in large pieces.

    d. A pigeon will see food that a cat or dog will not.

2. While the red light was on, Harvey walked around in circles and paced back and forth.

    a. Harvey liked to walk.

    b. Harvey knew that he would not get food when the red light was on.

    c. Harvey walked around in circles whenever the light changed.

    d. Harvey did not peck for food while the red light was on.

3. The researchers wanted to study Harvey's range of behaviors.

    a. Harvey did more than one thing.

    b. The researchers wanted to teach Harvey more things.

    c. Harvey could not learn.

    d. Harvey was a good experimental animal.

4. Something goes wrong, and we feel like striking out at those who are near us.

    a. We tend to blame others for bad things that happen.

    b. We do not handle our feelings very well.

    c. Handling anger is difficult for every person and every pigeon.

    d. We want to express our feelings.

    e. It is always dangerous to be around angry people.

    f. Feeling like striking does not mean that we strike out at others.

Finding the Main Ideas

Choose the best answer.

1. The main idea of this story:

   a. Researchers use pigeons for experiments to learn about animal behavior.

   b. The researchers learned about pigeons' ability to discriminate.

   c. We can learn a lesson about behavior from an experiment with a pigeon named Harvey.

   d. Pigeons are not like people.

2. The main idea of the moral of the story is:

   a. Pigeons do not like to be hungry.

   b. Pigeons make connections between the color of the light and success in getting food.

   c. Pigeons that seem to be frustrated have violent behavior.

   d. Red lights are not as good as green lights.

Reading for Details

Find the answers to these questions in the story.

1. When will a pigeon press a bar for food?

2. What is the meaning of a green light in the pigeon's cage?

3. What changes when the red light comes on?

4. How did the pigeon wait? (What did the pigeon do while he waited?)

5. Do animal psychologists think that a bird can be patient?

6. Why did Harvey kill the other bird?

7. Was Harvey the only violent pigeon?

8. What did Harvey seem to blame the other pigeon for?

Taking a Close Look at the Meaning of the Words

1. The words *discriminate*, *tell the difference*, *detect*, and *distinguish* are all about the same action. Here are the words in the same sentence:

   A person can talk about the differences between red and blue.

   A person can tell the difference between red and blue.

   A person can discriminate between red and blue.

   A person can detect the difference between red and blue.

   A person can distinguish red from blue. (no *between*)

2. The pigeon was *agitated*. The pigeon was *frustrated*. These sentences have verb forms in them. *To agitate* means to upset emotionally or physically. *To frustrate* means to deny someone something that he believes he should have. Both actions result in being angry.

3. *To blame someone* is to refuse to understand one's own responsibility. It is a normal human reaction. Good communication often depends on not blaming anyone.

Mary Gives to Marie

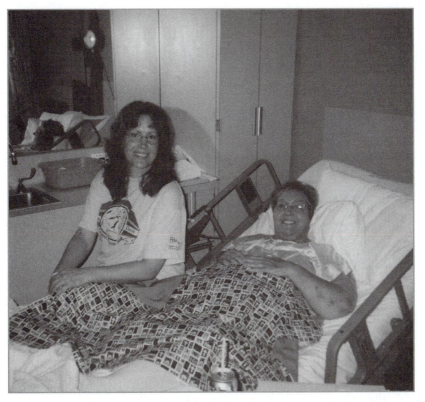

Marie's kidneys had failed. Her only hope for life was to get a kidney from another person. Her sister-in-law offered one of hers.

Before You Read the Story

Use these questions as preparation for reading the story. If you need to know the meaning of a word or idiom, check the Words and Idioms List after the story.

1. What do you know about the story from the pictures and the title?

2. What is a gift? What kind of gift is really valuable?

3. This is a story about a hero, or actually a heroine. A hero is a person who performs a great act. In this story a woman does something that needs courage. What is the act of courage?

4. What are the two stories of Mary and Marie? How are these two women alike?

5. Which is more difficult, the giving or receiving of a gift? Why?

While You Read the Story

Read these questions and look for the answers as you read the story.

1. What is Marie's medical problem?

2. Why has she had this problem for five years?

3. Why was Mary tested?

4. What was Mary's decision?

Mary Gives to Marie

1   The story is a simple one. Chris and Mary are both teachers. They fell in love, got married, and had three children, triplets. Their three children are the focus of their lives. Regina, Joel, and William are a wonder to watch. They are fraternal, not

5   identical, triplets. In other words, they look very different from one another. But they are very close friends as well as siblings. Watching their children makes

10   Mary and Chris aware of the importance of family. Closeness in their relationships has always  been important to them. In fact, getting together with aunts and uncles, nieces and nephews is their idea of fun.

15   The love between siblings is natural in the Giannola family. They both came from large families. Chris is one of six. Mary has a twin brother and nine other siblings. The brothers and sisters have always cared for one another. They have been supportive of the others' desires, goals, and dreams.

20   Then one day, disaster hit the family. Chris's brother-in-law Nick telephoned. Chris's sister Marie was in the hospital. She was very sick. Because her kidneys were too small, they had worked too hard. And now they were failing. It would be necessary for Marie to go on dialysis. That meant that for

25   four or five hours three times a week, she would have to go to a dialysis center. There a machine would clean her blood artificially. Dialysis is an expensive and painful process.

A person's body works because of the internal organs. The heart pumps the blood. Lungs add oxygen to the blood.

30 The stomach takes in the food and processes it. The intestines feed the blood with proteins and carbohydrates. Blood carries the food to the cells of the body. Blood also carries the wastes of the body to the two kidneys. In a normal person, the two kidneys clean the blood. They remove the poisons

35 and extra fluids from the blood. The liquid with these waste products goes to the bladder. From there it is then excreted as urine.

Marie's kidneys had shut down. The fluids in her body were no longer passing out normally. Because her kidneys

40 were not working anymore, she needed medical help. For five years, Marie had dialysis. Her life was very hard. Her family asked her doctor to help Marie because of the quality of her life.

The doctor said that her patient's only hope for a normal

45 life was a transplant. A healthy kidney would give her many more years of life. A person really needs only one kidney. Nature, it seems, gives every person a spare. However, not just any kidney will do. There are different blood types and different kinds of cell types. The giver, or donor, and the

50 receiver must match in blood and cell types. A member of a person's immediate family is the most likely kidney donor. So Chris and his brothers and sisters were tested. The whole family was sad because none of the immediate relatives could be donors. Where could they find a healthy kidney for

55 Marie? How can you ask a stranger to have major surgery and give up a kidney? Everyone was doubtful about finding a donor.

Then Mary said, "Test me." The doctor was skeptical because Mary and Marie are not blood relatives. They are

60 related by marriage. However, to everyone's surprise, the

tests came back positive. Mary and Marie were a match in blood and cells types. Mary's kidney would probably work normally in Marie's body. The lab did more testing. It should be possible for Mary's kidney to work for Marie.

65   Soon there were arrangements in a big Texas hospital. Mary and Marie would both be prepared for surgery. Marie would take special medicine so that her body would not reject a new kidney. The two women would check into the hospital at 70 the same time. They would have operations in adjoining operating rooms. They would be anesthetized at the same time. In one room, surgeons would prepare Marie for a new kidney. Meanwhile, in the other room, 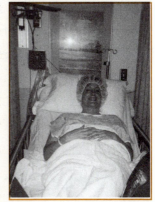 75 another team would remove one of Mary's healthy kidneys, and she would be closed up. Mary would go to "post-op" to recover under the watchful eyes of the nurses. Meanwhile, the doctors would sew Mary's healthy kidney into Marie. The doctors would have to watch to see that it 80 started to work. Then they would close up Marie and take her to post-op.

In post-op Chris and Nick saw Mary first. She was doing fine. Then the two men saw Marie. Even asleep from the anesthesia,  85 Marie looked better. Her skin looked pink and healthy. Only a few hours earlier she had looked gray. It seemed that this gift would make a difference.

If everything went along all right, Mary 90 would be able to leave the hospital in three days. Marie could be there a week longer.

The doctors would have to check on Mary's transplanted kidney several times a day. They wanted to make sure that Marie's body was not rejecting it. Mary left the hospital on 95 the fourth day. Marie came home only one day later. It was a miracle!

Now Marie can eat and drink anything. She can go where she wants to go. She has her life back, thanks to her incredibly generous sister-in-law, Mary.

100 Mary is back with her family, and Marie is back with hers. Mary's two kidneys are both working well. Furthermore, there is now a special relationship between the two sisters-in-law. They are related by much more than marriage.

Words and Idioms List

You already know some of these words and idioms. Go through the list. Write a check (✓) next to each of those that you do not know.

Some of these words and idioms may be completely new for you. Find them in the reading. Use the sentences around them to understand what they mean. Note how they are used. These are the words and idioms to learn for this story.

1. _____ **adjoining** (adjective): connecting; next-door

2. _____ to **anesthetize** (verb): to put to sleep with medicine

3. _____ **artificially** (adverb): not naturally; by machine

4. _____ to **be related** (verb): to be a relative

5. _____ a **bladder** (noun): a body organ where body liquids are held

6. _____ a **carbohydrate** (noun): a starch or a sugar in food

7. _____ **dialysis** (non-count noun): a blood-cleaning system for people whose kidneys do not work well

8. _____ to **excrete** (verb): to push out (of the body)

9. _____ a **fluid** (noun): a liquid

10. _____ **fraternal** (adjective): not identical

11. _____ **generous** (adjective): loving; not selfish

12. _____ **identical** (adjective): exactly the same

13. _____ **incredibly** (adverb): hard to believe

14. _____ **internal** (adjective): inside; within the body

15. _____ a **kidney** (noun): a body organ that removes waste from blood

16. _____ a **miracle** (noun): a happening that cannot be explained easily

17. _____ an **organ** (noun): a part of the body with one job to do

18. _____ a **protein** (noun): a food such as meat, cheese, or eggs

19. _____ to **pump** (verb): to cause a liquid to move through pipes

20. _____ to **reject** (verb): to throw away; to refuse to use

21. _____ to **shut down** (verb): to stop working

22. _____ a **sibling** (noun): a brother or sister

23. _____ **skeptical** (adjective): not willing to believe that something will happen

24. _____ a **spare** (noun): an extra one of something

25. _____ to **stomach** (noun): the body organ that accepts food

26. _____ **surgery** (non-count noun): an operation in which doctors try to fix a medical problem

27. _____ a **transplant** (noun): a person's organ that is put into the body of another person to replace one that isn't working

28. _____ **triplets** (plural noun): three children born of one mother at the same time

29. _____ **urine** (non-count noun): liquid waste from a human body

After You Have Read the Story

Do you have the answers to the questions from "While You Read the Story"? Talk about the answers with your classmates.

Understanding Sequence

In the blank in front of each sentence, write 2–12 to show that you know the order of the story.

a. _____ The search for a transplant started.

b. _____ Her blood relatives were tested, but none of them could give her a kidney.

c. __1__ Marie's kidneys shut down.

d. _____ The doctors said that Marie needed a transplant.

e. _____ The family asked Marie's doctors to help her improve her quality of life.

f. _____ Her sister-in-law Mary asked to be tested.

g. _____ Both women recovered from the surgery.

h. _____ The lab tests showed that Mary's and Marie's cell and blood types matched.

i. _____ One of Mary's healthy kidneys was removed from her body.

j. _____ Marie started dialysis to clean her blood and remove body fluids.

k. _____ Both women went back to their families.

l. _____ Marie received Mary's kidney in a transplant operation.

Answering Questions About the Story

Read these questions, think about the answers, and then discuss the answers with your classmates.

1. What are some of the organs of the human body?
2. What does each of those organs do in the body?
3. What does dialysis do?
4. How long does dialysis take?
5. What is a spare?
6. What two kinds of food does the blood carry to parts of the body?
7. Who are usually the best organ donors for a person?
8. Why was Marie's doctor skeptical about Mary as a possible kidney donor?
9. Why was Marie's doctor surprised by the tests on Mary's cell and blood types?
10. What was the result of the two operations?

Drawing Conclusions from the Story

Which of these statements are probably true, from the information in the story? Write *true* or *false* in the blank in front of each sentence.

1. _____ A kidney can be removed from one person and put inside another person.

2. _____ The cell and blood types of donor and receiver must match.

3. _____ Dialysis is a life-saving process.

4. _____ Dialysis is a long and painful process.

5. _____ Doctors try to improve quality of life for their patients.

6. _____ Marie's primary (main) doctor was a woman.

7. _____ A person can be healthy with just one kidney.

8. _____ Anyone can give another person a kidney.

9. _____ There are reasons that some people cannot be organ donors.

10. _____ There are several types of cells and blood.

Finding the Meaning in Context

A. Which meaning is closest to the underlined word or words? Circle *a, b, c,* or *d.*

1. Marie's doctor was <u>doubtful</u> about Mary as a transplant donor.
   a. careful
   b. pleased
   c. skeptical
   d. special

2. A medical <u>catastrophe</u> hit the family.
   a. disaster
   b. condition
   c. miracle
   d. circumstance

3. Kidneys remove waste material and extra body <u>fluids</u>.
   a. urine
   b. organs
   c. spares
   d. liquids

4. If something is <u>not natural</u>, it is probably done by machine.
   a. identical
   b. artificial
   c. fraternal
   d. skeptical

5. Mary's kindness and willingness to experience pain were <u>hard to believe</u>.
   a. skeptical
   b. generous
   c. incredible
   d. a miracle

B. Find the word or idiom in the Words and Idioms List that completes each sentence and write the correct form of it in the blank.

1. Body wastes are _____ from the body as

   _____ .

2. The _____ receives the food that a person eats and begins to process it.

3. Air, especially oxygen, is added to the blood by the _____ .

4. The _____ remove poisons from the blood and send the waste in fluids to the _____ .

5. The two kinds of food that the blood carries to the organs are _____ and _____ .

6. When something stops working, it _____ .

7. The kind of medicine that puts a person into a deep sleep is called _____ .

8. A person who is willing to give a great deal is a _____ person.

9. Two rooms that are next to each other, with a door between them, are _____ rooms.

10. Mary could be a donor for Marie because the tests for matching cell and blood types came back _____ .

Matching New Words and Meanings

A. Draw a line between the two words or phrases with similar meanings.

1. surgery	a. triplets
2. doubtful	b. carbohydrates
3. stop working	c. extra
4. internal	d. giver
5. siblings	e. operation
6. twins	f. shut down
7. fraternal	g. skeptical
8. spare	h. inside
9. donor	i. brothers and sisters
10. protein	j. not identical

B. Find the words in the two columns above that complete the sentences and write the correct form of each one in the blanks.

1. Both _____ and _____ mean "not sure."

2. Under ordinary circumstances, a person does not need an

   _____ or a _____ ; one is enough.

3. Twins can be _____ or _____ .

4. The word _____ means brothers and sisters together.

5. Two different kinds of food are _____ and

   _____ .

6. Multiple births can be either _____ or _____ .

7. The person who gives an organ for transplant is a _____

   or _____ .

8. Skin is an outside or external organ; the heart is an _____

   or _____ organ.

9. When a person's kidneys _____ , he or she must go

   on dialysis. A person cannot live long if his or her kidneys

   _____ .

10. To do a transplant _____ , there must be doctors to do

    two _____ , one for the donor and one for the receiver.

Practicing with Idioms

Find the idiom in this list that completes each sentence and write the correct form of it in the blank. Note that some words (for example, *[something]*) can be replaced with other words and might be in another position in the sentence.

to look gray	to make a difference
to check into	to be blood relatives
to be closed up	to have [something] back
to come from	to be related by marriage
to be back with	

1. When a person is sick, he or she might _____ .

2. Two brothers-in-law are _____ . That is, their relationship is legal and not through family.

3. The land was so dry that one entire day of rain didn't _____ for the farmers.

4. After three days, we _____ our lost puppy _____ . We thought it was gone forever.

5. The lost puppy _____ us now, after being gone for three days.

6. The triplets—Regina, William, and Joel— _____ . (They _____ the same family.)

7. On the day of the surgery, both Marie and Mary _____ the hospital at the same time.

8. After the surgeons removed a healthy kidney from Mary, she _____ and taken to post-op.

Understanding Family Relationships

Here is the list of family relationships: *aunt, brother, brother-in-law, cousin, daughter, father, grandmother, grandfather, husband, nephew, niece, sister, sister-in-law, son, uncle, wife.*

Find the word in the list above that answers each question in write it in the blank.

1. Who is Chris to…

   a. Marie? _____

   b. Mary? _____

   c. Regina? _____

   d. Nick? _____

2. Who is Mary to…

   a. William? _____

   b. Marie? _____

   c. Chris? _____

   d. her twin? _____

3. Who is Regina to…

   a. Joel? _____

   b. Chris? _____

   c. Mary? _____

   d. Marie? _____

   e. Nick? _____

4. Who is Marie to…

   a. Regina, William, and Joel? _____

   b. Chris? _____

   c. Mary? _____

5. Who is Nick to…

   a. Mary? _____

   b. Chris? _____

   c. William, Joel, and Regina? _____

Extra Question: Who is Marie to her doctor? _____

Exploring the Ideas

Think about these questions. Talk about your opinions with your classmates.

1. Marie did not want Mary to give her a kidney for a very good reason. What do you think the reason was? (Do you think Marie didn't want a healthy kidney?)

2. It is possible for organs from a person who has just died to be given to a living person. Some frequently transplanted organs are hearts, livers, hearts and lungs together, kidneys, and parts of the eyes. On a person's driver's license in many places, a person can write that he or she is willing to be an organ donor. How do you feel about this concept? Would you be willing to give your organs away when you no longer need them? Would you be willing to receive an organ from another person if you needed it to live?

3. There are many questions of ethics in transplant surgery. How do you feel about this topic? Transplant surgery saves lives. Is there more to think about than that fact?

4. Who should not be an organ donor? What reasons are good reasons not to consider a person as an organ donor?

Finding the Differences

What's the difference between…

1. an organ and a transplant?

2. a sister and a sister-in-law?

3. a brother and a sibling?

4. a nephew and a niece?

5. a fluid and a liquid?

6. surgery and an operation?

7. being asleep and being asleep from anesthesia?

8. a disaster and a miracle?

9. a giver and a donor?

10. twins and triplets?

Making Inferences

Read the numbered sentence. Then read the sentences under it. Which ones are true because the numbered sentence is true? Circle the letter in front of each true statement.

1. A person really needs only one kidney.

   a. One kidney will clean the blood for a person.

   b. A person should give one kidney away to someone else.

   c. Some people don't need any kidneys.

2. At a dialysis center, a person's blood can be cleaned by a machine.

   a. The dialysis machine is like an artificial kidney.

   b. A machine cannot do the work of a kidney.

   c. A dialysis machine is very small and easy to operate.

   d. Only a skilled person knows how to use a dialysis machine.

   e. A person who needs one can have a dialysis machine in his or her home.

3. Marie would take special medicine so that her body would not reject Mary's kidney.

   a. Without special medicine, a receiver's body would reject another person's kidney.

   b. There is medicine to stop rejection of organ transplants.

   c. It was possible that Mary's kidney would not work in Marie's body for a long time.

   d. Marie needed anti-rejection medicine before the surgery. (*Anti-* means "against.")

4. In post-op, even asleep from the anesthesia, Marie looked pinker and healthier than before the operation.

   a. Marie was pink and healthy in appearance before the surgery.

   b. Mary's kidney started to work immediately.

   c. It was obvious right away that Marie's new kidney was working.

   d. Marie was sicker after the operation than before it.

5. A donor and a receiver must have matching cell and blood types.

   a. A donor and a receiver are the same person.

   b. There are several different kinds of cell types among human beings.

   c. There are different blood types, and different people have different types.

   d. For every individual, there are a limited number of possible donors.

Finding the Main Ideas

Choose the best answer.

1. Which sentence is a summary of Mary's and Chris's families?

   a. They have fifteen brothers and sisters between them.

   b. They have very close relationships with all their siblings.

   c. Mary has a twin brother.

   d. The two families have a lot of children.

   e. Chris and Mary have good parents.

2. Which sentence best expresses the main idea of Mary and Chris's family?

   a. They are the Giannolas.

   b. There are triplets in the family.

   c. The members of the family are very close to one another.

   d. The three children are William, Joel, and Regina.

3. Which sentence best expresses the main idea of Marie's medical problem?

   a. Her kidneys did not work, so she needed dialysis.

   b. Her kidneys were smaller than normal.

   c. The quality of life for her was not good.

   d. She could not go on trips.

4. Which sentence best expresses the main idea of the surgery?

   a. Each of the two women had to have an operation.

   b. Mary had serious surgery to remove a kidney.

   c. The two women had surgeries at the same time.

   d. One of Mary's kidneys was transplanted into Marie.

5. What is the main idea of this story?

   a. A generous woman gave a kidney to her sister-in-law to save her life.

   b. Family relationships mean that one must love and support other members of the family.

   c. Dialysis is a painful and expensive process that can keep people alive.

   d. Having siblings is an important part of human experience.

Reading for Details

Find the answers to these questions in the story.

1. Who are Regina, Joel, and William?

2. How many siblings does Mary have?

3. What is the difference between fraternal twins?

4. What is the difference between identical twins?

5. How many brothers and sisters does Chris have?

6. How many kidneys does a human being have?

7. How many working kidneys does a human being need?

8. Why can't some people be organ donors?

9. Why was Marie's doctor skeptical about Mary as a donor for Marie?

10. Why did Marie have to take special medicine before her surgery? What did this medicine do? Did it work?

Taking a Close Look at the Meanings of the Words

1. The word *patient* is both an adjective and a noun. As an adjective, it means "willing to wait without bad feelings." Here is an example context:

    > The *patient* child waited until all the other children had asked their questions. Then he asked his question.

    The word *patient* is also a noun. It means "someone who is under the care of a doctor." Here are examples:

    > The doctor went to visit all her *patients* in the hospital every morning.

2. All *surgeons* are *doctors*, but not all *doctors* are *surgeons*. Under ordinary circumstances, only surgeons perform operations. It takes extra training to become a surgeon.

3. *Immediate relatives* are people who are blood relatives (mother, father, brother and sister.) For a donor, a sibling is the most likely to be a good donor. Siblings have more in common with one another than with one of their parents.

4. The words for relatives by marriage use hyphens: *brother-in-law, daughter-in-law, father-in-law, mother-in-law, sister-in-law,* and *son-in-law*. The plural of these nouns is made with an –*s*; however, the –*s* is added to the relationship word: *brothers-in-law, daughters-in-law, fathers-in-law, mothers-in-law, sisters-in-law,* and *sons-in-law*. The possessive is different: *brother-in-law's name, daughter-in-law's name, father-in-law's name, mother-in-law's name, sister-in-law's name,* and *son-in-law's name*.

Vocabulary List

Vocabulary List

Annotations		
n	→	noun
n pl	→	plural noun
v	→	verb
adj	→	adjective
adv	→	adverb
idiom	→	idiom

A

accumulation (n) 3
acre (n) 2
act out (v) 10
acupressure (n) 7
acupuncture (n) 7
adjoining (adj) 15
adrenaline (n) 8
adult (n) 2
affect (v) 13
aggressive (adj) 14
agitate (v) 14
airy (adj) 3
aisle seat (n) 1
ammonia (n) 3
ancestral ties (n pl) 8
anesthetize (v) 15
angel (n) 1
apologize (v) 13
arch (n) 3
argue (v) 5
armpit (n) 7
artificially (adv) 15
asparagus (n) 5

assemble (v) 11
assure someone (v) 7
attachment (n) 3
attack (v) 3
attic (n) 9
autumn (n) 2

B

baby (adj) 10
bait (n) 6
Balkans (n pl) 10
bank vault (n) 1
base (n) 13
basement (n) 9
beak (n) 14
be all smiles (idiom) 4
be aware (adj) 13
be beyond comfort (idiom) 9
beehive (n) 6
be in touch with (idiom) 6
belly (n) 6
bend, bent, bent (v) 7
be related (v) 15

be shocked (v) 1, 8
be speechless (idiom) 4
be worth it (idiom) 6
billboard (n) 8
bladder (n) 15
blame (v) 14
bleed, bled, bled (v) 8
blend in (v) 8
blooming (adj) 8
blurry (adj) 8
board a flight (idiom) 1
boil (v) 11
bolt (V) 2
booming (adj) 8
bouillon cube (n) 11
bowels (n) 7
bratwurst (n) 11
brawn (n) 2
bride (n) 1
brow (n) 13
brush up on (idiom) 10
bucket (n) 2
bump (n) 4
bureau (n) 3
burlap (n) 2
burst into laugher, burst, burst
    (idiom) 10
bushel basket (n) 6

C

canning factory (n) 2
can opener (n) 11
capital (n) 12
carbohydrate (n) 15
casserole (n) 11
catastrophe (n) 9
cemetery (n) 12

chance (n) 10
change a diaper (idiom) 1
charming (adj) 5
cheesecake (n) 11
chef (n) 11
Chemical Mace (n) 8
china closet (n) 3
choke (v) 8
choke something out (idiom) 10
chowder (n) 11
chunky (adj) 11
cinnamon (n) 3
cloudy (adj) 12
clue (n) 12
coffeecake (n) 11
coincidence (n) 1
collect (v) 6
comment on (v) 3
Communism (n) 8
complex (n) 4
concept (n) 13
confused (adj) 13
congestion (n) 7
connect (v) 14
connection (n) 14
consult (v) 11
continent (n) 10
corkscrew (n) 7
corridor (n) 8
cottage (n) 12
cottage cheese (n) 11
cranberries (n pl) 5
crime (n) 8
criminal (n) 8
crochet (v) 1
cushion (n) 3

D

dairy cow (n) 5
damp (adj) 3
dandelion (n) 6
date (n) 11
deduct (v) 2
defy (v) 7
deliver (v) 5
departure (n) 1
depressed (adj) 5
detect (v) 14
device (n) 10
dialysis (n) 15
diced (adj) 11
din (n) 2
direct route (idiom) 8
disagreement (n) 5
discard (v) 11
discrimination (n) 14
disinterested (adj) 13
dome (n) 4
doubt (n, v) 7
dough (n) 11
drain (n, v) 9, 11
drawer (n) 3
duffel bag (n) 1
drive something into something
　else, drove, driven (idiom) 1
drool (v) 8
drugged (adj) 1
dust (n) 3

E

earn (v) 2
effect (n) 13
eggs over easy (idiom) 11
elaborate (adj) 11
Ellis Island (n) 12

emphasize (v) 13
energy (n) 7
enlist (v) 5
enroll in (v) 5
eventually (adv) 14
evidence (n) 12
excrete (v) 15
excuse oneself (v) 13
experimentation (n) 13
explore (v) 10
eyesight (n) 14

F

feel welcome, felt, felt (idiom) 2
finance (n) 8
fish (v) 6
fishhook (n) 6
flap (v) 2
flash heater (n) 10
flock (n) 2
fluff up (v) 3
fluid (n) 15
forefathers (n pl) 12
fraternal (adj) 15
free afternoon (idiom) 12
free enterprise (n) 8
freeze, froze, frozen (v) 6
freshman (n) 13
from top to bottom (idiom) 9
frustrated (adj) 14
furnace (n) 6
furrow (v) 13

G

gather (v) 6
generous (adj) 15
glance (v) 1

gleaming (adj) 6
glove (n) 6
Goliath (n) 8
graduate (v) 5
grassy (adj) 2
grave (n) 12
gravity (n) 7
gravy (n) 5
greens (n pl) 6
greet (v) 10
greeting (n) 12
grinding sound (idiom) 4
grip (v) 13
groom (n) 1
guffaw (n) 10

H

harsh (adj) 5
have daggers in one's eyes (idiom) 1
hawk (n) 2
hearing impairment (n) 5
help at the house (idiom) 9
herd (n) 2
high noon (idiom) 2
hired help (n, idiom) 2
hitch (v) 6
hominy (n) 11
hood (n) 4
hoof, hooves (n) 2
hullabaloo (n) 2

I

identical (adj) 15
immigration (n) 12
impress someone (v) 10
incredibly (adv) 15
index finger (n) 7

ingredient (n) 11
insight (n) 2
intelligent (adj) 14
intend (v) 5
interact (v) 13
interfere (V) 14
internal (adj) 15

J

jar (n) 6
jungle (n) 13

K

keen (adj) 14
keep workers on the job (idiom) 9
kidney (n) 15
kneel, knelt, knelt (v) 2
knuckle (n) 13

L

laboratory (n) 14
lace (n) 1
law of nature (n) 7
layover (n) 1
lead (n) 9
leaky faucet (idiom) 9
lean (v) 9
leave something behind, left, left
   (idiom) 4
lectern (n) 13
lecture (n) 13
legal paper (n) 5
linoleum (n) 3
log (n) 6
loop (n) 7
lounge (n) 1
lung (n) 2

M

make something from scratch
  (idiom) 11
manage (v) 10
mar (v) 9
massage (n, v) 7
maternal (adj) 12
meadow (n) 2
medicine (n) 1
metal tub (n) 6
miracle (n) 15
miss someone (idiom) 12
mop (n) 3
moral (n) 14
motivation (n) 2
moussaka (n) 11
mugger (n) 8
mushroom (n) 11
mystery furniture (idiom) 10
mysterious (adj) 7

N

naïve (adj) 14
nature (n) 6
navy (n) 5
neutral (adj) 14
non-stop (adv) 1
nowhere to be found (idiom) 9
nutrient (n) 7

O

observe (v) 13
obvious (adj) 2
official (adj) 12
old country (idiom) 12
on the tip of one's tongue (idiom) 13
organ (n) 15
out of the blue (idiom) 4

P

pail (n) 2
pantry (n) 3
paramedic (n) 8
parish priest (n) 5
passenger seat (n) 4
pastor (n) 12
paternal (adj) 12
patient (n) 5
patiently (adv) 14
peck (v) 14
peel (v) 6
perfect (adj) 3
photograph album (n) 5
pickpocket (n) 8
pigeon (n) 14
pine knot (n) 6
pipe fitter (n) 9
pitch in (idiom) 11
planted (adj) 2
play a few notes (idiom) 3
plead, pleaded, pled (v) 4
pluck (v) 2
plug (n) 9
plugged drain (idiom) 9
plumber (n) 9
plump (adj) 6
poison (n) 1, 8
polish something (v) 3
porch (n) 3
postmark (n) 12
pots and pans (n) 3
precious (adj) 9
press (v) 14
pressure (n) 7
pressure cooker (n) 11
privacy (n) 8
procedure (n) 7

prompt (adj) 8
promptly (adv) 14
pros and cons (idiom) 8
protein (n) 15
psychologically (adv) 5
public address system (n) 1
pulsing (adj) 7
pump (v) 15

Q

quit claim (n) 5

R

rags (n) 3
react (v) 12
reaction (n) 13
realization (n) 5
recipe (n) 11
regular (adj) 7
reject (v) 15
researcher (n) 14
restrained (adj) 14
reward (n) 14
rights (n pl) 5
riot (n) 12
ripe (adj) 6
roadside (adj) 10
rob (v) 6
roots (n) 12
rose hip (n) 6
ruin (v) 1

S

sack (n) 2
salts (n) 7
salsa (n) 11
sauerkraut (n) 11

sausage (n) 11
saved by the bell (idiom) 12
scales (n pl) 6
science (n) 13
scrape (v) 6
scrub (v) 3
search (n) 12
sear meat (idiom) 11
senior citizen (n) 5
servant (n) 1
settle into a place (idiom) 12
shake out, shook, shaken (v) 3
shawl (n) 3
sheet (n) 3
shine, shone, shone (v) 3
shiny (adj) 4
shuffle (v) 8
shut down, shut, shut (v) 15
sibling (n) 15
side of the family (idiom) 12
silverware (n) 3
skeptical (adj) 15
slice (v, n) 11
slit, slit, slit (v) 6
slouch (v) 13
souvenir (n) 10
spare (n) 15
sparkle (v) 3
spider (n) 3
spirit (n) 8
spokesperson (n) 13
spot someone (idiom) 12
spotless (adj) 4
stab (v) 8
stare in disbelief (idiom) 10
stay put (idiom) 4
stem (n) 6

stew (n) 11
stick out, stuck, stuck (v) 8
sting (n) 6
stomach (n) 15
straighten (v) 3
strain (n) 7
stretch out (idiom) 2
strip (n) 1
stubbornly (adv) 2
subconscious mind (n) 13
subject (n) 14
substitution (n) 11
supervisor (n) 5
surgery (n) 15
surround (v) 2
susceptible (adj) 13
sweep, swept, swept (v) 3
switch off (v) 14

T

take care of something, took, taken
    (idiom) 4
target (n) 8
theory (n) 13
think for a moment, thought,
    thought (idiom) 9
thriving (adj) 4
thug (n) 8
thunderstorm (n) 2
toast (n) 11
town (n) 12
trailer (n) 6
transplant (n) 15
trash (n) 3
treasures (n) 1
triplets (n) 15
twist (v) 7

U

undaunted (adj) 5
understand supply and demand,
    understood, understood (idiom) 4
universe (n) 7
uprising (n) 12
urine (n) 15

V

vacuum (v) 3
veteran (n) 5
village (n) 12
violent (adj) 8
volunteer (n) 8
vulnerable (adj) 13

W

waiting room (n) 1
war-like (adj) 14
wash basin (n) 3
wash some things by hand (idiom) 9
water closet (n) 10
watercress (n) 6
wax (n) 6
whirring sound (idiom) 2
widow (n) 4
window sill (n) 3
wipe (v) 3
wooden rafter (n) 9
workshop (n) 7
wounded (adj) 5
wrinkled (adj) 5

Y

yearling (n) 2